COSMOGONIC REFLECTIONS

LUDWIG KLAGES

COSMOGONIC REFLECTIONS

Selected Aphorisms from Ludwig Klages

LONDON
ARKTOS
2015

ISBN 978-1-910524-41-1

BIC-CLASSIFICATION
Philosophy: metaphysics and ontology (HPJ)
Psychology (JM)

TRANSLATOR
Joseph D. Pryce

EDITORS
Jonathan Paquette and John B. Morgan

LAYOUT AND COVER DESIGN
Tor Westman

COVER ILLUSTRATION
Caspar David Friedrich, *The Monk by the Sea*
(German: *Der Mönch am Meer*), 1808–10.

ARKTOS MEDIA LTD.
www.arktos.com

Contents

Foreword

by Joseph D. Pryce

Soul and Spirit

The very title of Klages' metaphysical treatise, *Der Geist als Widersacher der Seele* (The Spirit as Adversary of the Soul), refers to the ceaseless and savage battle waged by Spirit against the soul. The mounting onslaught of Spirit against the living soul has constituted the innermost essence of the life of man. Whereas Spirit once existed in a temporary and uneasy symbiosis with the soul, in the course of human history, Spirit's destructive power waxes ever stronger, until Spirit eventually abandons the symbiotic compromise that endured whilst the powers of life were still exalted, and erupts into the waning empire of the living soul as a savage and unyielding demon whose malevolent career reaches its grisly climax in our apocalyptic age of "virtual" reality, compassion-babble, hydrogen bombs, and racial chaos.

But just what is this "soul?" In the first place, the soul is not something exclusively human, for all phenomena possess soul, such as the sea, animals, mountains, the wind, and the stars. In fact, all phenomena are "en-souled." The soul possesses two poles, the archetypal soul and the substantial soul, or, to look upon these matters from a slightly different angle, a passive receptor pole and an active effector pole. The passive receptor pole is, in the thought of Klages, the truly characteristic aspect for the soul's life. From its birth, the soul leads a pathic, or passive, dream-existence, in which its life is filled with visionary images. The soul only becomes released for activity in the phenomenal world when the bearer of that soul is confronted by the polarity of another soul, which forces each soul to reveal its nature to the other. The original characteristics of the soul are night, dreaming, rhythmic pulsation, infinite distance, and the realm of the unconscious.

The "elementary" substances that constitute the earth originated under the complex influence of telluric and cosmic forces, and the symbiotic interaction of all telluric phenomena was required in order to bring the animate world into being. According to the doctrine of the "actuality of the images," the plant represents the transitional stage between the element and the living creature. (The botanist Jagadis Bose performed experiments that he felt conclusively demonstrated the capacity of plants to experience pain). The plant experiences life in the form of growth and maturation, as well as in the creation of offspring through the processes familiar to natural science. Spontaneous movements of various kinds are characteristic of plant-life, such as the turning of the leaves and buds to the light, the sending of the root-system into the soil in order to extract nourishment from the earth, the fixing of supportive tendrils to fixed surfaces, and so on. Klages draws our attention to the fact that there are several varieties of plant that are indubitably capable of self-motility. There are, at this threshold of another realm of being, organisms such as sea squirts, mussels, oysters, sponges, and zoophytes, which become fixed in their habitat only after the early stages of the lives. (When Verworrn published his experiments on the psychical life of the protista in 1899, he attributed sensation to these organisms, a position that certainly has much to recommend it. But when he attempted to demonstrate that even the will is in evidence at this stage of life, one can only shake one's head in disbelief, for that which this author adduces as evidence of volition in the protista is the simple phenomenon of reaction to stimuli! Thus, Verworrn equates the reactive responses in the protista to the action of the will in man, in whom the "volitional" processes are more highly developed. This is certainly a case of blindness to a difference of essence.)

In the next developmental stage, i.e., that of the animal, the soul is now captured in a living body. The drives and instincts make their first appearance during this phase. The characteristic functions of the creature comprise physical sensation (as represented by the body-pole) and contemplation (the psychical pole). The living body is the phenomenon of the soul, and the soul is the meaning of the living body. However, in opposition to the realm of the lower animals, wherein sensation dominates contemplation, we find that in the higher animals, contemplation is strengthened at the expense of the physical sensations, as the result of Spirit's invasion of the life-cell, which occurs at this time. If one were to consider "the waking state" to be synonymous with consciousness itself, than one must conclude that consciousness is present in animal and man alike. According to Klages, however, it is only the capacity for conceptual thought that characterizes consciousness, so that we must attribute consciousness proper only to man. In the animal, the image cannot be divorced from the sensory impression. In man, on the other hand, the content of the visual image can be separated from the act of perception that receives that content through the sensorium. Therefore, although the animal undoubtedly possesses instincts, only man is truly conscious.

The biological processes that constitute plant and animal life are also operative in man, but with the intervention of Spirit (at least during the initial phase of development, during which Spirit and life maintain some kind of balance), he is capable of creating symbolic systems of communication and expression, such as art and poetry, as well as myth and cult. The processes of life establish the polar connection between the actual images of the world (or, the "macrocosm") and the pathic soul that receives them (or, the "microcosm"). The *human* soul comprises the totality of the immediate experiences of man. It is the soul that receives its impressions of actuality in the shape of images. "The image that falls upon the senses: that, and nothing besides, is the meaning of the world," Klages insists, and one such immediate act of reception can be seen in the manner in which one comprehends the imagery employed by a great poet or the skillfully drawn portrait executed by a gifted artist. The actualities received by the "pathic" soul are experienced in the dimensions of space and time, but they have their coming-to-be and their passing-away solely within the temporal order. In sharp contrast to the traditional Christian insistence that virtue constitutes a valorization of the "Spirit" at the expense of a denigrated body, Klages sees man's highest potential in the state of ecstasy, such as in the privileged state of rapture in which the connected poles of body and soul are liberated from the intrusive "Spirit." What the Christian understands by the word *soul* is, in fact, actually *Spirit*, and *Spirit* — to simplify our scheme somewhat for the sake of expediency — is the mortal *adversary of the soul.* Another way to express this insight would be the formula: *Spirit is death, and soul is life.*

Spirit manifests its characteristic essence in formalistic cognition and technological processes, and in the hyper-rationalism that has pre-occupied Western thought since the Renaissance. Both mathematical formalism and "high" technology have reared their conceptual skyscrapers upon a foundation formed by the accumulation of empirical data. Spirit directs its acolytes to the appropriation and rigidification of the world of things, especially those things that are exploitable by utilitarian technocrats. Spirit fulfills its project in the act, or event, that occurs within the spatio-temporal continuum, although Spirit itself has its origin outside that continuum. Spirit is manifest in man's compulsive need to seize and control the materials at hand, for only "things" will behave consistently enough for the Spirit-driven utilitarian to be able to "utilize" them by means of the familiar processes of quantification and classification, which enable "science" to fix, or "grasp," the thing in its lethal conceptual stranglehold.

We must draw a sharp distinction between the thing and its properties on one side, and the "essence" (*Wesen*) and its characteristics on the other. Only an essence, or nature, can be immediately experienced. One cannot describe, or "grasp," an essence by means of the conceptual analysis that is appropriate only when a scientist or technician analyzes a thing in order to reduce it to an "objective" fact that will submit to the grasp of the concept. The souls of all phenomena unite to comprise a world of sensuous images, and it is only as unmediated images that the essences appear to the pathic soul who receives their meaning-content. The world of essences (*phenomena*) is experienced by the pathic soul, which is the receptor of the fleeting images that constitute actuality (*Wirklichkeit der Bilder*). These images wander eternally in the restless cosmic dance that is the Heraclitean flux. The image lives in intimate connection with the poles of space and time.

The world of things, on the other hand, is rationally comprehended as a causally connected system of objects (noumena). In the course of historical time man's ability to perceive the living images and their attendant qualities is progressively impoverished until Spirit finally replaces the living world of expressive images with the dead world of mere things, whose only connections are adequately expressed in the causal nexus, or, to use the language of science, the "laws of nature."

In the final act of the historical tragedy, when there is no longer any vital substance upon which the vampire spirit may feed, the parasitic invader from beyond time will be forced to devour itself.

Paradise Lost

We see that the philosophy of Klages has both a metaphysical dimension as well as a historical one, for he sees the history of the world as the tragic aftermath to the disasters that ensued when man was expelled from the lost primordial paradise in which he once enjoyed the bliss of a "Golden Age." When man found himself expelled from the eternal flux of coming-to-be and passing-away of the lost pagan paradise, he received in exchange the poor substitute known as consciousness. Paradise was lost, in effect, when man allowed his temporally-incarnated life-cell to be invaded by the a-temporal force that we call Spirit.

Klages is quite specific in putting forward a candidate for this "Golden Age" which prospered long before Spirit had acquired its present, murderous potency, for it is within the pre-historic Aegean culture-sphere, which has often been referred to by scholars as the "Pelasgian" world, that Klages locates his vision of a peaceful, pagan paradise that was as yet resistant to the invasive wiles of Spirit.

Who are these "Pelasgians," and why does the Pelasgian "state of mind" loom so largely in Klages' thought? According to the philosopher, the development of human consciousness, from life, to thought, to will, reveals itself in the three-stage evolution from prehistoric man (the Pelasgian), through the Promethean (down to the Renaissance), to the Heraclitean man (the stage which we now occupy). For Klages, the Pelasgian is the human being as he existed in the prehistoric "Golden Age" of Minoan Crete, Mycenean Hellas, and the related cultures of the Aegean world. He is a passive, "pathic" dreamer, whose predominant mode of being is contemplation. He consorts directly with the living Cosmos and its symbols, but he is doomed.

The "Pelasgians" occupy a strategic place in the mythos of Ludwig Klages, and this "Pelasgian Realm" of Klages closely resembles the mythic Golden Age of Atlantis that looms so large in the *Weltanschauung* of E. T. A. Hoffmann. But who, in fact, were these Pelasgians? According to the prehistorians and mythologists, the Pelasgians were an ancient people who inhabited the islands and seacoasts of the eastern Mediterranean during the Neolithic and Bronze Age periods. Homer, in a well-known passage in the *Odyssey* (XIX, 175 ff), places them on Crete, but another writer, Dionysius Halicarnassus, could only tell us that the Pelasgians were *autokhthonoi*, or "indigenous" throughout Hellas. Homer also refers to "Lord Zeus of Dodona, Pelasgian," in the *Iliad* (II, 750). Plutarch says of them that "they were like the oak among trees: the first of men at least

in Akhaia," while Pliny believes that Peloponnesian Arkadia was originally called Pelasgis; that Pelasgos was an aristocratic title; and that the
Pelasgians were descended from the daughters of Danaos.

The most famous Pelasgian settlement was at Dodona, and Thucydides
(we discover with relief) informs us that *all Greece was Pelasgian before the
Trojan war* (approximately 1200 BCE): "Before the Trojan War no united
effort appears to be made by Hellas; and to my belief that name itself had
not yet been extended to the entire Hellenic world. In fact, before the time
of Hellen, son of Deucalion, the appellation was probably unknown, and
the names of the different nationalities prevailed locally, the widest in
range being 'Pelasgians.'"[1] Homer mentions them in the *Iliad* (II, 840),
and, in the *Odyssey* (XIX, 172-177), the poet describes them as "divine."
Racially, there seems to be no doubt that the Pelasgians were an Aryan
people, and physical anthropologists inform us that the twenty skulls discovered at the Minoan sites of Palakaistro, Zakro, and Gournia turn out
to be predominantly dolicocephalic, with the cranial indices averaging
73.5 for the males, and 74.9 for the women.[2] The historian Herodotus, like
Thucydides, groups all of the pre-Classical peoples of the Hellenic world
under the name Pelasgian: "Croesus made inquiries as to which were the
greatest powers in Hellas, with a view to securing their friendly support,
and, as a result of these inquiries, he found that the Lacedaemonians and
the Athenians stood out among the people of the Dorian and Ionian race
respectively. Of these people that had thus made their mark, the latter
was originally a Pelasgian and the former a Hellenic nationality... As regards the language spoken by the Pelasgians, I have no exact information;
but it is possible to argue by inference from the still-existing Pelasgians
who occupy the city of Creston in the hinterland of the Tyrrhennians;
from the other Pelasgians who have settled in Placia and Scylace on the
Hellespont; and from the various other communities of Pelasgian race

---

1   Book I of the *History of the Peloponnesian War*, Oxford text, edited by H. Stuart-
    Jones; translated by Arnold J. Toynbee.
2   R. W. Hutchinson, *Prehistoric Crete* (Harmondsworth: Penguin Books, 1962).

which have changed their national name. If inferences may be legitimately drawn from this evidence, then the original Pelasgians were speakers of a non-Greek language, and the Athenian nation must have learned a new language at the time when they changed from Pelasgians into Hellenes. At all events, the inhabitants of Creston and of Placia, who in neither case speak the same language as their present respective neighbors, do speak the same language as one another…In contrast to this, the Hellenic race has employed an identical language continuously, ever since it came into existence. After splitting off from the Pelasgian race, it found itself weak, but from these small beginnings it has increased until it now includes a number of nationalities, its principal recruits being Pelasgians It is my further opinion that the non-Hellenic origin of the Pelasgians accounts for the complete failure of even this nationality to grow to any considerable dimensions."[3] The rest, as they say, is silence (at least in the Classical sources), and we can see why this obscure people should appeal to the mythologizing "Golden Age" bent of Klages. Modern authorities regard the Pelasgians as inhabitants of a purely *Neolithic* culture pertaining only to the area of Thessaly bounded by Sesklo in the east and the Peneios valley in the west (the area which is now known as Thessaliotis).

Although the philosopher's alluring portrait of the Pelasgians was formulated before modern archaeology had completed our image of Aegean prehistory, the picture which Klages paints, in the Eros-book and in the "Magna Mater" chapter of *Der Geist als Widersacher der Seele*, of a vibrant, healthy, and physically beautiful people, in touch with the gods and with nature, requires little — if any — correction in the wake of the new researches. The figures who move so gracefully through the enchanted atmosphere of the palace frescoes at Knossos, as they carry their brightly-colored gifts of vase, flowers, and *pyxis*, to the Goddess, are straight out of a poet's dream. This Minoan, or "Pelasgian," world was characterized by a dialectical fusion of two strains of religiosity: on the one hand, we meet with the Aegean worship of the Mother Goddess, with all that that entails

---

3   Herodotus, Book I, chapters 56 to 58.

with regard to ritual and style of living; and, on the other, we confront the Indo-European sky-god, or Father God, and the two strains seem to co-exist in an uneasy, unstable — but certainly fruitful — truce. Mythologists tell us that this heritage is reflected in the tales that indicate the marriages between the Indo-European sky-god Zeus with various incarnations of the Aegean Mother Goddess (in some of the myths, Zeus is, himself, born on Crete!). In time, of course, the Father God will achieve dominance in the Hellenic world, but Klages is more interested in traces of the religion of the Goddess as it survives from the Stone Age into the world of the second millennium BCE.

Our philosopher, in effect, merges the misty Neolithic and Bronze Age cultures of the ancient Aegean into a single magical world-space, wherein an innocent race lives at one with Nature and the Goddess. Klages treats the Pelasgians as *the primeval Hellenes*, who worshiped the Goddess, as she was embodied in female idols in the form of figurines of the famous steatopygous Fertility-Goddess type, with huge belly and swollen but-tocks (even though this iconographic image, represented most clearly in the *Venus of Willendorf*, proceeds from a much earlier cultural stratum, the Palaeolithic. The later Greeks celebrated Demeter, the Life-Mother, in the Eleusinian mysteries). The palace culture of Minoan Crete would ex-emplify the matriarchalist style of the (late) Pelasgian world, especially as prehistoric Knossos had a far more sophisticated attitude toward women than did, say, the later Periclean Athens. For instance, in the legend of Ariadne, the fact that her presence is indicated at the funeral games shows us that women were free to mingle with men at their will, and the version of the myth which shows Ariadne as in charge of the palace in her father's absence shows the great value which the Cretans placed on women. This centrality of woman is indicated in all of Minoan art, which depicts her as beautifully-animated; in fact, one of the most elegant of the ebon-tressed, slim-waisted, and crimson-lipped women depicted on the frescoes on the Palace of Knossos, was nicknamed *La Parisienne* by a French visitor at the turn of the century!

Klages is drawn more toward the "pacifist," thalassocratic (sea-ruling) aspect of the Minoans of the second millennium BCE, than toward the covetous Bronze Age Greeks of the mainland with their heavily-fortified cities and unending wars (the Bronze Age mainlanders seem to have loved war for its own sake; another troubling element in their civilization is their reliance on slavery, especially of women). These are the Mycenaeans, who would eventually sack, and destroy, the Minoan culture. It is a notable fact that most of our evidence about the "Pelasgian" religious beliefs and practices stems from Minoan Crete: very little material survives from Mycenae and the other mainland sites. On Crete, however, we find the dove-goddess image and the snake-goddess image, the stepped altars and shrine models, in religious sanctuaries overflowing with such sacred items. Clearly, the Goddess ruled on Minoan Crete, and, in fact, the Goddess Potnia, whose name crops up repeatedly in the Linear B tablets, might indeed be the "Lady of the Labyrinth," which is to say, the Lady of the Place of the *labrys*, or the double ax — the Palace of Knossos itself. Another Knossos cult-figure was the *anemo ijereja*, of "Priestess of the Winds"; there is also *qerasija*, which could well mean "the Huntress." According to some historians, offerings to the Goddess were entirely bloodless, and were usually gifts of honey, oil, wine, and spices like coriander and fennel; sheep and their shepherds were associated with Potnia, but certainly not in the aspect of blood-sacrifices. On the mainland, however, we find the Mycenaeans slaughtering rams, horses, and other animals in their vaulted tombs. We also find the cult of the Goddess on the Cycladic islands (to which "Greek islands" American "millionaires" and other arch-vulgarians habitually cart their flatulent girths on "vacations"). The famous Cycladic figurines represent the Mother Goddess as well, under the aspects of "the divine nurse" or the "Goddess of Blessing." In these figurines the Goddess is almost invariably represented with the pubic delta and the stomach emphasized.

In the early phase of Minoan religion, the relationship of ruler and deity was not that of father-and-son, but of *mother-and-son*. For Minoan

Crete, the Mother Goddess was represented on earth by the priest-king. Some lovely manifestations of this reverence for the Goddess can be found in the faience statuettes of the bare-breasted Mother Goddess which were found by Sir Arthur Evans in the Palace of Knossos: one of them shows the Goddess holding up a serpent in each of her hands; the other statuette shows the snakes entwining themselves around her arms. These figures appear in both "peak sanctuaries" and in household shrines, and have been designated by prehistorians as the "Snake Goddess" or the "Household Goddess." The "Household Goddess" is often associated with the motif of the double-axe, the emblem of the Palace at Knossos, and also with the horns of consecration, which associate her with the sacred bull of the Palace of King Minos. One inhabitant of the Palace of King Minos was the princess Ariadne, to whom we alluded briefly above. After the loss of Theseus, the fate of Ariadne would be intimately intertwined with that of Dionysus, the problematic Greek divinity whose cult excited so much controversy and such fierce opposition among the Greeks of the Classical Age.

Dionysus was the orgiastic god in whom Klages, following Nietzsche, locates the site of an untrammeled sensuous abandon. This Thraco-Grecian deity, whose nature was so brilliantly interpreted by Nietzsche in the latter half of the nineteenth century, and by his worthy successor Walter F. Otto in the first half of the twentieth century, becomes the ultimate symbol of heathen life in the Klagesian view, the epiphany of that frenzied ecstasy that the god's followers achieved by means of the drunkenness and wild dancing of the maenads, those female adherents of the god of the vine, who experienced genuine enthusiasm, i.e., "the god within," as they followed the progress of their far-wandering god, who gave to man the inestimable gift of wine. These maenads celebrated their secret Dionysian cultic rituals far from the accustomed haunts of man, and any man was slaughtered on the spot if he should be apprehended whilst illicitly witnessing the ceremonies reserved for the gods' female followers. These maenads were alleged to be in the possession of magical powers that enabled the god's worshipers to bring about magical effects at great distances. And "all Eros is Eros of distance!"

Philosophical Roots and Biological Consequences

Der Geist als Widersacher der Seele contains a comprehensive survey of the philosophical literature that relates to "biocentric" concerns, and in these pages Klages closely scrutinizes the troubled seas and fog-shrouded moorlands of philosophy, both ancient and modern, over which we, unfortunately, have only sufficient time to cast a superficial and fleeting glance. We will, however, spend a profitable moment or two on several issues that Klages examined in some detail, for various pivotal disputes that have preoccupied the minds of gifted thinkers from the pre-Socratics down to Nietzsche were also of pre-eminent significance for Klages. One of the pre-Socratic thinkers in particular, Heraclitus of Ephesus (c. 536-470 BCE), the "dark one," was looked upon by Ludwig Klages as the founding father of "biocentric," or life-centered, philosophy. Klages and Heraclitus share the conviction that life is ceaseless change, chaos, "eternal flux" (*panta rhei*). Both thinkers held that it is not matter that endures through the ceaseless patterns of world-transformation: *it is this ceaseless transformation itself* that is the enduring process, which alone constitutes this ever-shifting vibrancy, this soaring and fading of appearances, this becoming and passing away of phenomenal images upon which Klages bestowed the name *life*. Likewise, Klages and Heraclitus were in complete accord in their conviction that natural events transpire in a succession of rhythmical pulsations. For both thinkers, nothing abides without change in the human world, and in the cosmos at large, everything flows and changes in the rhythmical and kaleidoscopic dance that is the cosmic process. We cannot say of a thing: "it is"; we can only say that a thing "comes to be" and that it "passes away." The only element, in fact, in the metaphysics of Heraclitus that will be repudiated by Klages is the great pre-Socratic master's positing of a "*logos*," or indwelling principle of order, and this slight disagreement is ultimately a trivial matter, for the *logos* is an item which, in any case, plays a role so exiguous in the Heraclitean scheme as to render the notion, for all practical and theoretical purposes, nugatory as far as the basic thrust of the philosophy of the eternal flux. Another great Greek philosopher, Protagoras of Abdera (c. 480-410 BCE), is fulsomely acclaimed by Klages as the "father of European psychology and history's pioneer epistemologist." When Protagoras asserted that the content of perception from moment to moment is the result of the fusion of an external event (the world) with an inner event (the experiencing soul), he was, in effect, introducing the Heraclitean flux into the sphere of the soul. No subsequent psychologist has achieved a greater theoretical triumph. The key text upon which Klages bases this endorsement is Sextus Empiricus' *Outlines of Pyrrhonism* I (217): "...matter is in flux, and as it flows additions are made continuously in the place of the effluxions, and the senses are transformed and altered according to the times of life and to all the other conditions of the bodies." (218) "Men apprehend different things at different times owing to their differing dispositions; for he who is in a natural state apprehends those things subsisting in matter which are able to appear to those in a natural state, and those who are in a non-natural state the things which can appear to those in a non-natural state." Thus, the entire sphere of psychical life is a matter of perception, which comprises the act of perception (in the soul) and the content of perception (in the object).

This Protagorean insight forms the basis for the distinction between *noumenon* and *phenomenon* that will exert such a fructifying influence on Western thought, especially during the period of German Romanticism. Greek thought has a significant bearing on crucial discoveries that were made by Klages. We have learned that there are two forces that are primordially opposed to each other, Spirit and life; in addition, we have seen these forces cannot be reduced to each other, nor can they be reduced to any third term; body and soul constitute the poles of unified life, and it is the mission of Spirit to invade that unity, to function as a divisive wedge in order to tear the soul from the body and the body from the soul. Thus,

Spirit begins its career as the disrupter of life; only at the end of history will it become the *destroyer* of life. We find a piquant irony in the oft-expressed view that accuses Klages of inventing this "Spirit" out of whole cloth, for those who have sneered at his account of the provenance of Spirit as a force that enters life from outside the sphere of life, dismissing the very idea from serious consideration by reducing the concept to a caricature ("Klagesian devil," "Klages with his Spirit-as-'space-invader,'" and so on), offer quite an irresistible opening for a controversialist's unbuttoned foil, because such statements reveal, at one and the same time, an ignorance of the history of philosophy in our professors and commentators that should curdle the blood of the most trusting students, as well as an almost incomprehensible inability, or unwillingness, to understand a scrupulously exact and closely-argued text. This intellectual disability possesses, one must confess, a certain undeniable *pathos*. As it happens, the question as to the provenance of Spirit has always enjoyed a prominent position in the history of philosophical speculation (especially in the narrow field of epistemology, i.e., the "theory of cognition"), and the Klagesian viewpoint that has been so ignorantly and persistently excoriated is explicitly drawn from the philosophy of — Aristotle! It was Aristotle, "the master of those who know," who, in discussing the divided substance of man, discovered that he could only account for the origin of one of the components, Spirit (Greek *nous*), by concluding that Spirit had entered man "from outside"! Likewise, the idea of a "tripartite" structure of man, which seems so bizarre to novice students of biocentrism, has quite a respectable pedigree, for, once again, it was Aristotle who viewed man as having three aspects: Psyche-Soma-*nous* (body-soul-Spirit). The speculations of the Greek philosophers who belonged to the Eleatic School provided the crucial insights that inspired Klages' masterful formulation of the doctrine of the "actuality of the images."

The specific problem that so exercised the Eleatics was the paradox of motion. The Eleatics insisted that motion was inconceivable, and they proceeded from that paradoxical belief to the conclusion that *all* change is impossible. One of the Eleatics, Zeno, is familiar to students of the history of philosophy as the designer of the renowned "Zeno's Paradoxes," the most famous of which is the problem of Achilles and the Tortoise. Zeno provided four proofs against the possibility of motion:

1. a body must traverse in finite time an infinite number of spaces and, therefore, it can never begin its journey;

2. this is Zeno's application of his motion-theory to the "Achilles" problem that we've just mentioned — if Achilles grants a lead or "head start" (analogous to a "handicap") to the tortoise against whom he is competing in a foot-race, he will never be able to overtake the tortoise, because by the time Achilles has reached point A (the starting point for the tortoise), his opponent has already reached point B. In fact, Achilles will never even reach point A, because before he can traverse the entire distance between his starting-point and point A, he must necessarily cover one-half of that distance, and then one-half of the remaining distance, and so on and so on *ad infinitum*, as it were;

3. the arrow that has just been launched by the archer is always resting, since it always occupies the same space; and

4. equivalent distances must, at equivalent velocity, be covered in the identical time. But a moving body will pass another body that is moving in the opposite direction (at the identical velocity) twice as quickly as when this body is resting, and this demonstrates that the observed facts contradict the laws of motion.

Betraying a certain nervousness, historians of philosophy usually dismiss the Eleatics as superficial skeptics or confused souls, but they never condescend to provide a convincing refutation of their "obvious" or "superficial" errors. Klages, on the other hand, finds both truth and error in the Eleatics' position. From the standpoint of an analysis of *things*, the Eleatics are on firm ground in their insistence on the impossibility of change, but from the standpoint of an analysis of *appearances*, their position is utterly false. Their error arose from the fact that the Greeks of this period had already succumbed to the doctrine that the world of appearances is a world of deception; a reservoir of illusory images. This notion has governed almost every metaphysical system that has been devised by Western philosophers down to our own time, and with every passing age, the emphasis upon the world of the things (noumena) has increased at the expense of the world of appearances (phenomena). Klages, on the other hand, will solve the "problem of the Eleatics" by an emphatic demonstration that the phenomenal images are, in fact, the only realities.

During the Renaissance, in fact, when ominous temblors were heralding the dawn of our "philosophy of the mechanistic apocalypse," there were independent scholars (among whom we find Giordano Bruno and Paracelsus) who speculated at length on the relationship that exists between the macrocosm and the microcosm, as well as on the three-fold nature of man and on the proto-characterological doctrine of the "temperaments." But the key figure in the overturning of the triadic world-view is undoubtedly the French thinker and mathematician René Descartes (1596-1650), who is chiefly responsible for devising the influential schematic dualism of thinking substance and extended substance, which has dominated, in its various incarnations and permutations, the thinking of the vast majority of European thinkers ever since. Descartes explicitly insists that all of our perceptions as well as every "thing" that we encounter must be reduced to the status of a machine; in fact, he even suggests that the whole universe is merely a vast mechanism (*terram totumque hunc mundum instar machinæ descripsi*). It is no accident, then, that Cartesian thought is devoid of genuine psychology, for, as he says in the *Discourse on the Method*, man is a mere machine, and his every thought and every movement can be accounted for by means of a purely mechanical explanation.

Nevertheless, there have been several revolts against Cartesian dualism. As recently as two centuries ago, the extraordinarily gifted group of "nature philosophers" who were active during the glory days of German Romanticism, pondered the question of the "three-fold" in publications that can be consulted with some profit even today. We have seen that the specifically Klagesian "triad" comprises body-soul-Spirit, and the biocentric theory holds that life, which comprises the poles of body and soul, occurs as processes and events. Spirit is an intruder into the sphere of life, an invader always seeking to sever the poles, a demonic willfulness that is characterized by manic activity and purposeful deeds. "The body is the manifestation of the soul, and the soul is the meaning of the living body."

We have seen that Klages was able to trace proleptic glimpses of this biocentric theory of the soul back to Greek antiquity, and he endeavored for many years to examine the residues of psychical life that survive in the language, poetry, and mythology of the ancient world, in order to interpret the true meanings of life as it had been expressed in the word, cult, and social life of the ancients. He brilliantly clarifies the symbolic language of myth, especially with reference to the cosmogonic Eros and the Orphic Mysteries. He also explores the sensual-imagistic thought of the ancients as the foundation upon which objective cognition is first erected, for it is among the Greeks, and only among the Greeks, that philosophy proper was discovered. During the peak years of the philosophical activity of the Greek thinkers, Spirit still serves the interests of life, existing in an authentic relationship with an actuality that is sensuously and inwardly "en-souled" (*beseelt*). The cosmological speculation of antiquity reveals a profound depth of feeling for the living cosmos, and likewise demonstrates the presence of the intimate bonds that connect man to the natural world; contemplation is still intimately bound up with the primordial, elemental powers. Klages calls this "archaic" Greek view of the world, along with its later reincarnations in the history of Western thought, the "biocentric" philosophy, and he situates this mode of contemplation as the enemy of the "logocentric" variety, i.e., the philosophy that is centered upon the *logos*, or "mind," for mind is the manifestation of Spirit as it enters Western thought with the appearance of Socrates.

From Plato himself, through his "neo-Platonic" disciples of the Hellenistic and Roman phases of antiquity, and down to the impover-

ished Socratic epigones among the shallow "rationalists" of seventeenth
and eighteenth century Europe, all philosophers who attempt to restore
or renew the project of a philosophical "enlightenment," are the heirs of
Socrates, for it was Socrates who first made human reason the measure
of all things. Socratic rationalism also gave rise to ethical schemes that
were alien to life, being based upon a de-natured creature, as in the idea of
man-as-such. This pure Spirit, this distilled ego, seeks to sever all natural
and racial bonds, and as a result, "man" prides himself upon being utterly
devoid of nobility, beauty, blood, and honor. In the course of time, he
will attach his fortunes to the even more lethal spiritual plague known
as Christianity, which hides its destructive force behind the hypocritical
demand that we "love one's neighbors." From 1789 onwards, a particularly
noxious residue of this Christian injunction, the undifferentiating respect
for the ghost known as "humanity," will be considered the hallmark of
every moral being.

The heirs of the Socratic tradition have experienced numerous instances of factional strife and re-groupings in the course of time, although
the allegiance to Spirit has always remained unquestioned by all of the
disputants. One faction may call itself "idealistic" because it considers
concepts, ideas, and categories to be the only true realities; another faction may call itself "materialistic" because it views "things" as the ultimate
constituents of reality; nevertheless, both philosophical factions give their
allegiance, *nolentes volentes*, to the Spirit and its demands. Logocentric
thought, in fact, is the engine driving the development of the applied science that now rules the world. And by their gifts shall ye know them! The
bitterly antagonistic attitude of Klages towards one of the most illustrious heirs of Socrates, Immanuel Kant, has disturbed many students of
German thought who see something perverse and disingenuous in this
opposition to the man whom they uncritically regard as the unsurpassed
master of German thought.

Alfred Rosenberg and the other official spokesmen of the National
Socialist movement were especially enraged by the ceaseless attacks on

Kant by Klages and his disciple, Werner Deubel. Nevertheless, Kant's pre-eminence as an epistemologist was disputed as long ago as 1811, when Gottlob Ernst Schulze published his *Critique of Theoretical Philosophy*, which was then, and remains today, the definitive savaging of Kant's system. Klages endorses Schulze's demonstration that Kant's equation: actuality = being = concept = thing = appearance (or phenomenon) is utterly false, and is the main source of Kant's inability to distinguish between perception and representation. Klages adds that he finds it astonishing that Kant should have been able to convince himself that he had found the ultimate ground of the faculty of cognition in — *cognition*!

Klages cites Nietzsche's *Beyond Good and Evil* with approval, in which Kant is ridiculed for attempting to ground his epistemology in the "faculty of a faculty"! Klages shows that the foundation of the faculty of cognition lies not in cognition itself, but in experience, and that the actuality of space and time cannot have its origins in conceptual thought, but solely in the vital event. There can be no experienced colors or sounds without concomitant spatio-temporal characteristics, for there can be no divorce between actual space and actual time. We can have no experience of actual space without sensory input, just as we have no access to actual time without thereby participating in the ceaseless transformation of the phenomenal images. Formalistic science and its offspring, advanced technology, can gain access only to a small segment of the living world and its processes. Only the *symbol* has the power to penetrate all the levels of actuality, and of paramount importance to Klages in his elaborate expositions of the biocentric metaphysics is the distinction between conceptual and symbolic thought.

We have previously drawn attention to the fact that drive-impulses are manifest in expressive movements that are, in turn, impelled by the influence of a non-conceptual power that Klages calls the symbol. Likewise, symbolic thinking is a tool that may profitably be utilized in the search for truth, and Klages contrasts symbolic contemplation with the logical, or "formalistic," cognition, but he is at pains to draw our attention to the errors into which an unwarranted, one-sided allegiance to *either* type of thought can plunge us. Although Klages has been repeatedly and bitterly accused by Marxists and other "progressives" as being a vitriolic enemy of reason, whose "irrationalism" provided the "fascists" with their heaviest ideological artillery, nothing could be further from the truth. On occasions too numerous to inventory, he ridicules people like Bergson and Keyserling, who believe that "intuition" lights the royal road to truth. His demolition of the Bergsonian notion of the *élan vital* is definitive and shattering, and his insistence that such an entity is a mere pseudo-explanation is irrefutable, and might have been published in a British philosophical journal. In the end, Klages says, "irrationalism" is the spawn of— *Spirit!* Our ability to formulate and utilize concepts as well as our capacity to recognize conceptual identities is sharply opposed to the procedure involved in the symbolic recognition of identities.

The recognition of such conceptual identities has, of course, a crucial bearing on the life of the mind, since it is this very ability that functions as the most important methodological tool employed by every researcher involved in the hard sciences. Symbolic identification, on the other hand, differs widely from its conceptual counterpart in that the symbolic type derives its meaning-content from the "elemental similarity of images." Thus, the process of substantive, or conceptual, identification confronts its opposite number in the "identity of essence" of symbolic thought. It is this "identity of essence," as it happens, which has given birth to language and its capacity to embody authentic meaning-content in words. Jean Paul was quite right, Klages tells us, in describing language as a "dictionary of faded metaphors," for every abstraction that is capable of verbal representation arose from the essentiality of the meaning-content of words. He draws a sharp distinction between the true symbol (Greek *symbolon*, i.e., token) and the mere sign whose significance is purely referential. The true meaning of an object resides in its presence, which Klages refers to as an *aura,* and this aura is directly communicated to a sensory apparatus that resists all purely linguistic attempts to establish formulas of equivalence or "correspondence."

The sensual imagination participates in an unmediated actuality, and intuitive insight (*Schauung*) allows us to gain access to a realm of symbols, which rush into our souls as divine epiphanies. Life resists rules, for life is eternal flux. Life is not rigid being, and therefore life will always evade the man-traps of mind, the chains of the concept. Life, comprising the poles of body and soul, is the physical event as phenomenal expression of the soul. There can be no soul-less phenomena and there can be no souls without (phenomenal) appearances, just as there can be no word-less concepts and no words without meaning content. The physical world is the image-laden appearance (phenomenon) that manifests a psychical substance. When the demonic object encounters the receptive, or "pathic," soul, the object becomes a symbol and acquires a "nimbus," which is a pulsating radiance surrounding the moment of becoming. This nimbus is referred to as an "aura" when applied to persons, and both nimbus and aura represent the contribution of the object to the act of perception. Non-symbolic, formalistic thought, on the other hand is irreverent, non-contemplative, and can best be characterized as an act that is enacted in the service of Spirit, which imperiously and reductively ordains that the act of perception must also be an act of the will. Thus the will attains primacy even over the de-substantialized intellect, and Klages — who has persistently been dismissed as an obscurantist and irrationalist — never misses an opportunity to re-iterate his deep conviction that *the essence of Spirit is to be located in the will and not in the intellect.*

As we've seen, Klages holds that the living soul is the antithesis of the Spirit. The Spirit seeks to rigidify the eternal flux of becoming, just as the soul, in yielding passively to the eternal flux, resists the raging Heraclitean spirit and its murderous projects. Body and soul reach the peak of creative vitality when their poles are in equipoise or perfect balance, and the high point of life is reached in the experience of sensuous joy. Spirit's assault upon the body is launched against this joy, and in waging war against the joy of the body, Spirit also wages war against the soul, in order to expel the soul, to make it homeless, and in order to annihilate all ecstasy and creativity.

Every attempt that has been made by monistic thinkers to derive the assault on life from the sphere of life itself has misfired. Such troublesome anomalies as the supernatural visions and cases of demonic possession that transpired during the Middle Ages, as well as the crippling cases of hysteria so familiar to psychologists in our own time, can never be satisfactorily explained unless we realize that the souls of these unfortunates were sundered by the acosmic force of Spirit, whose very essence is the will, that enemy and murderer of life. The conceptual "Tower of Babylon" reared by monists in their ludicrous efforts to derive the force that wages war against life from life itself is no less absurd than would be the foredoomed attempt of a firefighter to extinguish a blaze by converting a portion of the fire into the water that will extinguish the fire!

There is, however, one privileged example of a manifestation of the will in the service of life, and this occurs when the will is enlisted for the purposes of artistic creation. The will, Klages insists, is incapable of creative force, but when the artist's intuition has received an image of a god, the will functions "affirmatively" in the destructive assaults of the artist's chisel upon the marble that is to embody the image of the divinity. Actuality (the home of the soul) is experienced; being (the home of Spirit) is thought. The soul is a passive surrender to the actuality of the appearances. Actuality is an ever-changing process of coming to be and passing away that is experienced as images. Spirit attempts to fix and to make rigid the web of images that constitutes actuality by means of conceptual thought, whose concrete form is the apparatus of the scientist. Cognition represents identical, unfaltering, timeless being; life is the actuality of experience in time. When one says of time that it "is," as if it were something rigid and identical behind the eternal flux, then time is implicitly stripped of its very essence as that which is "temporal"; it is this temporal essence which is synonymous with becoming and transformation. When one speaks of a thing or a realm that is beyond, i.e., that "transcends," the unmediated, experienced actuality of the living world, one is merely misusing thought in order to introduce a conceptual, existential world in the place of the actual one, which has the inalienable character of the transitory and temporal. It is within the "pathic" soul that the categories of space and time originate. Acosmic Spirit, on the other hand, invaded the sphere of life from outside the spatio-temporal cosmos.

Klages scorns the schemes of philosophical "idealists" who attempt to ground the structures of space and time in some transcendental world. He also distinguishes a biocentric non-rational temporality from "objective" time. Biocentric thought, true to its immanentist ("this-worldly") status, recognizes that the images that pulsate in immanentist time are excluded by their very nature from any participation in objective time, for the images can only live within the instantaneous illumination of privileged moments. Klages savages the platitudes and errors of logocentric thinkers who adhere, with almost manic rigidity, to the conventional scheme of dual-axis temporality. In ordinary logic, time is viewed as radiating from the present (that extensionless hypostasis) backward into time-past and forward into time-to-come: but the whole scheme collapses in a heap as soon as we realize that the future, the "time-to-come," is nothing but a delirious void, a grotesque phantom, a piece of philosophical fiction. Only the past possesses true actuality; only the past is real. The future is merely a pale hallucination flitting about in deluded minds. True time is the relationship that binds the poles of past and present. This union occurs as a rhythmical pulsation that bears the moment's content into the past, as a new moment is generated, as it were, out of the womb of eternity, that authentic depository of actual time. Time is an unending cycle of metamorphoses utterly unrelated to the processes of "objective" time. True time, cyclical time, is clocked by the moments that intervene between a segment of elapsed time and the time that is undergoing the process of elapsing. Time is the soul of space, just as space is the embodiment of time. Only within actual time can we apprehend the primordial images in their sensuous immediacy.

Logic, on the other hand, can only falsify the exchange between living image and receptive soul. Let us examine the biological — or, more properly, *ethological* — implications of the doctrine of "primordial images" (*Urbilder*). Bear in mind, of course, the crucial distinction that is drawn by Klages between the science of fact (*Tatsachenwissenschaft*) and the science of appearances (*Erscheinungswissenschaft*): factual science establishes laws of causality in order to explain, e.g., physiological processes or the laws of gravitation; thus, we say that factual science examines *the causes of things*. The science of appearances, on the other hand, investigates the *actuality of the images*, for images are the only enduring realities. The enduring nature of the image can be seen in the example of the generation of a beech tree. Suppose a beech tree sheds its seed upon the forest floor, in which it germinates. Can we say of the mother tree that it lives within the child? Certainly not! We can chop down the mother tree and burn it to ashes, whilst the offspring continues to prosper. Can we say that the matter of which the old tree was composed survives intact within the younger tree? Again, no: for not an atom of the matter that made up the seed from which the young beech grew exists within it. Likewise, not an atom of the matter of which a man's body is composed at the age of thirty survives from that same man's body as it was on his tenth birthday.

If it is not the matter of which the organism is composed which endures through the ages, what then is it that so endures? "The one possible answer is: an image." Life and its processes occur outside the world of things. On the contrary: life comprises the events in the world of the images. Thus, we see that the doctrine of the "actuality of the images" (*Wirklichkeit der Bilder*) holds that it is not things, but images, that are "en-souled" (*beseelt*), and this proposition, Klages tells us, forms the "key to his whole doctrine of life (*Lebenslehre*)." Things stand in a closed chain of causality, and there is no reciprocal action between the image and the thing, no parallelism, and no connection, and the attempts that have been undertaken by various philosophers to equate the thing and the image merely serve to rupture the chain of causality in its relevant sphere, i.e., the quantitative scientific method. The receptive soul is turned towards the actuality of the image, and when we say on one occasion that an object is "red," and on another that this same object is "warm," in the first case the reference is to the reality of things, whereas in the second case the reference is to the actuality of images. By using the name of a color, we indicate that we are differentiating between the superficial qualities, or surface attributes, of things; when we say that a colored object is "warm" or "cold," on the other hand, we are pointing to the phenomenal "presence" that has been received by the pathic soul. In fact, there are a whole host of common expressions in which this attribution of subjective, psychical states to visible phenomena occurs. We say, for instance, that red is "hot" and that blue is "cold."

In the *Vom Wesen des Bewusstseins* (1921), a treatise on the nature of consciousness, Klages adduces an astonishingly vast inventory of words that are routinely utilized in descriptions of *subjective* as well as *perceptual* phenomena. Someone will speak of his a "bitter" feeling of resentment at some slight or injury. The expression that love is "sweet" occurs in almost every language. Likewise, joy is often described as "bright," just as grief or sorrow are often referred to as "dark." We also have "hot" anger (or the familiar variant, the "'heat' of the moment"). Images are the charged powers, or natures, that constitute the basis of all phenomena of cosmic and elemental life as well as of cellular, organic life. All that exists participates in the life of the images. Air, fire, earth, and water; rocks, clouds, planets and suns; plant, animal and man: all of these entities are alive and have souls that share in the life of the cosmos. It isn't matter that constitutes the stuff of reality, for matter perishes; but the image, which remains alive as it wanders through the rhythmically pulsating cosmos, never dies. It changes through the processes of maturation and growth in the organism, and it transforms itself through the millennia in the species. The images alone have life; the images alone have meaning. The souls of those who now live are images that are temporarily wedded to matter, just as the souls of the dead are images that have been released from matter. The souls of the dead revisit us in their actual form in dreams (*Wirklichkeitsform der Traumerscheinung*), unconstrained by the limitations of material substance. The souls of the dead are not expelled from the world to live on as immortal "Spirits" housed in some transcendent "beyond"; they are, instead, demonically vital presences, images that come to be, transform themselves, and vanish into the distance within the phenomenal world that is the only truly existing world. The human soul recalls the material palpability of the archaic images by means of the faculty that Klages calls "recollection," and his view in this regard invites comparison with the Platonic process of "anamnesis." The recollection of which Klages speaks takes place, of course, without the intervention of the will or the projects of the conscious mind.

Klages' examination of "vital recollection" was greatly influenced by the thought of Wilhelm Jordan, a nineteenth century poet and pioneer Darwinist, whose works were first encountered by the young philosopher at the end of that century. In Jordan's massive didactic poem *Andachten*, which was published in 1877, the poet espouses a doctrine of the "memory of corporeal matter." This work had such a fructifying influence on the thought of Klages that we here give some excerpts:

It is recollection of her own cradle, when the red stinging fly glues grains of sand into a pointed arch as soon as she feels that her eggs have ripened to maturity. It is recollection of her own food during the maggot-state when the anxious mother straddles the caterpillar and drags it for long distances, lays her eggs in it, and locks it in that prison. The larva of the male stag-beetle feels and knows by recollection the length of his antlers, and in the old oak carves out in doubled dimensions the space in which he will undergo metamorphosis. What teaches the father of the air to weave the exact angles of her net by delicate law, and to suspend it from branch to branch with strings, as firm as they are light, according to her seat? Does she instruct her young in this art? No! She takes her motherly duties more lightly. The young are expelled uncared-for from the sac in which the eggs have been laid. But three or four days later the young spider spreads its little nest with equal skill on the fronds of a fern, although it never saw the net in which its mother caught flies. The caterpillar has no eye with which to see how others knit the silken coffins from which they shall rise again. From whence have they acquired all the skill with which they spin so? Wholly from inherited recollection. In man, what he learned during his life puts into the shade the harvest of his ancestors' labors: this alone blinds him, stupefied by a learner's pride, to his own wealth of inherited recollections. The recollection of that which has been done a thousand times before by all of his ancestors teaches a new-born child to suck aptly, though still blind. Recollection it is which allows man in his mother's womb to fly, within the course of a few months, through all the phases of existence through which his ancestors rose long ago. Inherited recollection, and no brute compulsion, leads the habitual path to the goal that has many times been attained; it makes profoundest secrets plain and open, and worthy of admiration what was merely a miracle. Nature makes no free gifts. Her commandment is to gain strength to struggle, and the conqueror's right is to pass this strength on to his descendants: her means by which the skill is handed down is the memory of corporeal matter."

The primordial images embody the memory of actual objects, which may re-emerge at any moment from the pole of the past to rise up in a rush of immediacy at the pole of the present. This living world of image-laden actuality is the "eternal flux" (*panta rhei*) of Heraclitus, and its cyclical transformations relate the present moment to the moments that have elapsed, and which will come around again, *per sæcula sæculorum.*

Thus we see that the cosmos communicates through the magical powers of the symbol, and when we incorporate symbolic imagery into our inmost being, a state of ecstasy supervenes, and the soul's substance is magically revitalized (as we have already seen, genuine ecstasy reaches its peak when the poet's "polar touch of a pathic soul" communicates his images in words that bear the meaning of the actual world within them).

When prehistoric man arrives on the stage, he is already experiencing the incipient stages of the fatal shift from sensation to contemplation. Spirit initiates the campaign of destruction: the receptor-activity is fractured into "impression" and "apperception," and it is at this very point that we witness, retrospectively, as it were, the creation of historical man. Before the dawn of historical man, in addition to the motor processes that man possessed in common with the animal, his soul was turned towards wish-images. With the shift of the poles, i.e., when the sensory "receptor" processes yield power to the motor "effector" processes, we witness the hypertrophic development of the human ego. Klages is scornful of all egoism, and he repeatedly expressed bitter scorn towards all forms of "humanism," for he regards the humanist's apotheosis of the precious "individual" as a debased kowtowing before a mere conceptual abstraction. The ego is not a man; it is merely a *mask*. In the place of psychical wishes, we now have aims. In the ultimate stages of historical development, man is exclusively devoted to the achievement of pre-conceived goals, and the vital impulses and wish-images are replaced by the driving forces, or interests. Man is now almost completely a creature of the will, and we recall that it is the will, and not the intellect, that is the characteristic function of Spirit in the Klagesian system. However, we must emphasize that the will is not a creative, originating force. Its sole task is to act upon the bearer of Spirit, if we may employ an analogy, in the manner of a rudder that purposively steers a craft in the direction desired by the navigator. In order to perform this regulative function, i.e., in order to transform a vital impulse into purposeful activity, the drive impulse must be inhibited and then directed towards the goal in view.

Spirit in man is dependent upon the sphere of life as long as it collaborates as an equal partner in the act of perception; but when the will achieves mastery in man, this is merely another expression for the triumph of Spirit over the sphere of life. In the fatal shift from life to Spirit, contemplative, unconscious feeling is diminished and rational judgment and the projects of the regulative volition take command. The body's ultimate divorce from the soul corresponds to the soullessness of modern man whose emotional life has diminished in creative power, just as the gigantic political state-systems have seized total control of the destiny of earth. Spirit is hostile to the demands of life. When consciousness, intellect, and the will to power achieve hegemony over the demonic forces of the cosmos, all psychical creativity and all vital expression must perish.

When man is exiled from the realm of passive contemplation, his world is transformed into the empire of will and its projects. Man now abandons the feminine, unconscious mode of living and adheres to the masculine, conscious mode, just as his affective life turns from bionomic rhythm to rationalized measure, from freedom to servitude, and from an ecstatic life in dreams to the harsh and pitiless glare of daylight wakefulness. No longer will he permit his soul to be absorbed into the elements, where the ego is dissolved and the soul merges itself with immensity in a world wherein the winds of the infinite cosmos rage and roar. He can no longer participate in that *Selbsttödung*, or self-dissolution, which Novalis once spoke of as the "truly philosophical act and the real beginning of all philosophy." Life, which had been soul and sleep, metamorphoses into the sick world of the fully conscious mind. To borrow another phrase from Novalis (who was one of Klages' acknowledged masters), man now becomes "a disciple of the religion of philistines that functions merely as an opiate."

Man finally yields himself utterly to the blandishments of Spirit in becoming a fully conscious being. Klages draws attention to the fact that there are two divergent conceptions of the nature of consciousness in popular parlance: the first refers to the inner experience itself; whilst the second refers to the observation of the experience. Klages only concerns himself with consciousness in the second sense of the word. Experiences are by their very nature unconscious and non-purposive. Spiritual activity takes place in a non-temporal moment, as does the act of conscious thought, which is an act of Spirit. Experience must never be mistaken for the cognitive awareness of an experience, for as we have said, consciousness is not experience itself, but merely thought about experience. The "receptor" pole of experience is sharply opposed to the "effector" pole, in that the receptive soul receives sensory perceptions: the sense of touch receives the perception of "bodiliness"; the sense of sight receives the images, which are to be understood as pictures that are assimilated to the inner life. Sensation mediates the experience of (physical) closeness, whilst intuition receives the experience of distance. Sensation and intuition comprehend the images of the world. The senses of touch and vision collaborate in sensual experience. One or the other sense may pre-dominate, i.e., an individual's sense of sight may have a larger share than that of touch in one's reception of the images (or vice versa), and one re-ceptive process may be in the ascendant at certain times, whilst the other may come to the fore at other times. (In dreams the bodily component of the vital processes, i.e., sensation, sleeps, whilst the intuitive side remains wholly functional. These facts clearly indicate the incorporeality of dream images as well as the nature of their actuality. Wakefulness is the condition of sensual processes, whilst the dream state is one of pure intuition.)

Pace William James, consciousness and its processes have nothing to do with any putative "stream of consciousness." That viewpoint ignores the fact that the processes that transpire in the conscious mind occur solely as interruptions of vital processes. The activities of consciousness can best be comprehended as momentary, abrupt assaults that are deeply disturbing in their effects on the vital substrata of the unity of body and soul. These assaults of consciousness transpire as discrete, rhythmically pulsating "intermittencies" (the destructive nature of Spirit's operations can be readily demonstrated; recall, if you will, how conscious volition can interfere with various bodily states: an intensification of attention may, for instance, induce disturbances in the heart and the circulatory system; painful or onerous thought can easily disrupt the rhythm of one's breathing; in fact, any number of automatic and semi-automatic somatic functions are vulnerable to Spirit's operations, but the most serious dis-turbances can be seen to take place, perhaps, when the activity of the will cancels out an ordinary, and necessary, human appetite in the interests of the will. Such "purposes" of the will are invariably hostile to the organism and, in the most extreme cases, an over-attention to the dictates of Spirit can indeed eventuate in tragic fatalities such as occur in terminal sufferers from *anorexia nervosa*).

Whereas the unmolested soul could at one time "live" herself into the elements and images, experiencing their plenitudinous wealth of content in the simultaneous impressions that constitute the immediacy of the image, insurgent Spirit now disrupts that immediacy by disabling the soul's capacity to incorporate the images. In place of that ardent and erotic surrender to the living cosmos that is now lost to the soul, Spirit places a satanic empire of willfulness and purposeful striving, a world of those who regard the world's substance as nothing more than raw material to be devoured and destroyed.

The image cannot be spoken, it must be lived. This is in sharp contradistinction to the status of the *thing*, which is, in fact, "speakable," as a result of its having been processed by the ministrations of Spirit. All of our senses collaborate in the communication of the living images to the soul, and there are specific somatic sites, such as the eyes, mouth, and genitalia, that function as the gates, the "sacred" portals, as it were, through which the vital content of the images is transmitted to the inner life (these somatic sites, especially the genitalia, figure prominently in the cultic rituals that have been enacted by pagan worshipers in every historical period known to us).

An Age of Chaos

In the biocentric phenomenology of Ludwig Klages, the triadic historical development of human consciousness, from the reign of life, through that of thought, to the ultimate empire of the raging will, is reflected in the mythic-symbolic physiognomy which finds expression in the three-stage, "triadic," evolution from "Pelasgian" man — of the upper Neolithic and Bronze Ages of pre-history; through the Promethean — down to the Renaissance; to the Heracleic man — the terminal phase that we now occupy, the age to which two brilliant twentieth century philosophers of history, Julius Evola and Savitri Devi, have applied the name "Kali Yuga," which in Hinduism and Buddhism is the dark age of chaos and violence that precedes the inauguration of a new "Golden Age," when a fresh cycle of cosmic events dawns in bliss and beauty.

And it is at this perilous juncture that courageous souls must stiffen their sinews and summon up their blood in order to endure the doom that is closing before us like a mailed fist. Readers may find some consolation, however, in our philosopher's expressions of agnosticism regarding the ultimate destiny of man and earth. Those who confidently predict the end of all life and the ultimate doom of the cosmos are mere swindlers, Klages assures us. Those who cannot successfully predict such mundane trivialities as next season's fashions in hemlines or the trends in popular music five years down the road can hardly expect to be taken seriously as prophets who can foretell the ultimate fate of the entire universe!

In the end, Ludwig Klages insists that we must never underestimate the resilience of life, for we have no yardstick with which to measure the magnitude of life's recuperative powers. "All things are in flux." That is all.

EDITOR'S NOTE

This volume is the second in a series of translations of selections from Klages' oeuvre. A more detailed introduction to Klages' life and work is provided in the first volume, *The Biocentric Worldview.*

These texts were selected from several of Klages' works, and are denoted at the end of each text with the following abbreviations (all authored by Klages unless otherwise indicated):

AC   = *Zur Ausdruckslehre und Charakterkunde* (Heidelberg: Niels Kampmann, 1926)

AG   = *Ausdrucksbewegung und Gestaltungskraft* (Munich: Deutscher Taschenbuch Verlag, 1968)

LK GL = Hans Eggert Schröder, *Ludwig Klages: Die Geschichte Seines Lebens*, 3 vols. (Bonn: H. Bouvier, 1966-1992)

PEN   = *Die psychologischen Errungenschaften Nietzsches* (Leipzig: J. A. Barth, 1926)

RR   = *Rhythmen und Runen* (Leipzig: J. A. Barth, 1944)

SW   = *Sämtliche Werke*, 15 vols. (Bonn: H. Bouvier, 1965-1992)

Text in brackets was added by the translator for clarification. The footnotes were added by the editors.

Unfortunately, the current political climate necessitates this disclaimer, which should be a given but which must nevertheless be stated for the sake of clarity: the views expressed herein are those of the author, and do not necessarily reflect those of Arktos Media or the members of its staff.

JOHN B. MORGAN
Budapest, Hungary
June 2015

Selected Aphorisms
from Ludwig Klages

UNIVERSAL MORALITY. A man who cannot climb a tree will boast of never having fallen out of one. (RR p. 466)

DOWNFALL. Today, those are outstanding spirits indeed in whom one can expect to find any independence of judgment. The great masses, who have never been, in the history of mankind, more subject to hypnotic suggestion than they are right now, have become the puppets of the "public opinion" that is engineered by the newspapers in the service, it need hardly be emphasized, of the reigning powers of finance. What is printed in the morning editions of the big city newspapers is the opinion of nine out of ten readers by nightfall. The United States of America, whose more rapid "progress" enables us to predict the future on a daily basis, has pulled far ahead of the pack when it comes to standardizing thought, work, entertainment, etc.

Thus, the United States in 1917 went to war against Germany in sincere indignation because the newspapers had told them that Prussian "militarism" was rioting in devilish atrocities as it attempted to conquer the world. Of course, these transparent lies were published in the daily rags because the ruling lords of Mammon knew that American intervention in Europe would fatten their coffers. Thus, whereas the Americans thought that they were fighting for such high-minded slogans as "liberty" and "justice," they were actually fighting to stuff the money bags of the big bankers. These "free citizens" are, in fact, mere marionettes; their freedom is imaginary, and a brief glance at American work-methods and leisure-time entertainments is enough to prove conclusively that *l'homme machine* is not merely imminent: *it is already the American reality.*

Racial theorists seem cognizant of the fact that this will be the downfall of the white race, and that of the black and yellow races shortly thereafter. (Of the so-called "primitive" races, we say nothing other than that the few surviving tribal cultures are already at death's door!) All of these facts are scarcely relevant, since the ultimate destruction of all seems to be a foregone conclusion. It is not this destruction that makes us sorrowful here, for no prophet can foretell whether a completely robotic mankind will survive for centuries, or even for millennia: what concerns us is the mechanization process itself. It is the tragic destiny of knowledge — of authentic knowledge and not of the imaginary sort, which provides the intellectual implements required by engineers and technicians — that it performs the funeral march that accompanies the disappearance, if not the burial, of a living essence. The only thing that we know is that we are no more. "*Somnium narrare vigilantis est*" (Seneca). (SW 4 pp. 408–9)

ON THE PSYCHOLOGY OF THE DRIVES. We are dealing here with a subject about which, bluntly speaking, nothing but a load of nonsense has hitherto been expounded. We have, in fact, said very little when we note that a psychology of the drives simply does not exist, because what has already been said on this topic, and said far too many times, demonstrates such a fundamental falsification of the facts that no further proof of the sheer ignorance of our ruling authorities is required. At least that is our impression when we turn our attention away from the pointless experimental research of today to the rich achievements of Romantic philosophy, and to the still considerable, but undoubtedly lesser, philosophical achievement of Nietzsche, whose deeply probing views on the drives were linked from the outset to his presentation of the "will to power" as it affects vital processes. Let us now attempt a comprehensive illumination of the drives, by means of a refutation of one well-known and suggestive point of view that has become a sort of classic example.

Those psychologists who have blinded themselves to the very concept of life and who still insist on investigating the drives, regardless of whether they proceed intentionally like [Theodor] Lipps, the dissector of consciousness, or whether, on the contrary, their purpose is to interpret volitional impulses as strictly analogous to drive impulses, like the thinker Schopenhauer, will always interpret them by analogy with the *will*. If these psychologists lack any insight into the essential difference which obtains between drive impulses and volitional impulses, then, since it is a rare thing for man to experience drive impulses without experiencing concomitant volitional impulses, they will, without fail, transport Spirit [*Geist*] into the non-conscious drives and will misconstrue the drives in the worst conceivable fashion at the very moment when they are attempting to interpret acts of will in terms of pure drive impulses. Because the will pursues purposes, the life impulse, in its turn, is also conceived as purposive, and, in the end, the whole of nature is interpreted as if it were a systematic constellation of purposes. Now, because volitional impulses are realized in achievements, and because we have grown accustomed to deducing the former from the latter, instead of the drives themselves, certain *consequences arising from their activation,* are studied, which are then imputed to the drives as intentions that are directed towards the achievement of an effect. Thus, since only an "ego" is capable of willing, i.e., an "ego" which asserts itself in every act of willing, the interest of the bearer of the will in its own self-preservation is transformed into a self-preservation drive possessed by all animate creatures.

Perhaps a few examples will help to clarify this problem. Our domesticated animals eat and drink just as we do. Although they don't know, we do know, that nobody could survive at all, were that person to give up eating and drinking completely. And so we are conscious of nutritive purposes and are enabled to make decisions such as the decision to improve our diet or the decision to desist from unnecessary gourmandizing; and the conclusion that has been drawn from this realization is that eating and drinking are primordial and universal functions of a nutritive drive, and that in this nutritive drive, it is the self-preservation drive that is forcefully announcing its presence.

Now if someone were to say: but animals do not have the slightest idea that in order to live they have to take in calories; for even were we to assume that they are, in fact, capable of acquiring this knowledge, this would not dispose of the obvious fact that they perform these so-called purposive actions before they acquire it (e.g., the chick, which having just emerged from its egg, immediately pecks at the corn); nor, indeed, are these purposive actions restricted to the consumption of food, for they comprise a thousand and one other functions as well (e.g., the exodus of the migratory birds in the autumn). At this point, the faithful disciple of the self-preservationist creed, of *sacro egoismo,* will in all candor parade those phrases which, after they have been stripped of subterfuge and obfuscation, announce that all these phenomena are due to non-purposive purposes, thought-less thoughts, and unconscious consciousness! Just who is thinking here and who is not? The "self-preserving" creature does not think, but its inborn "nature" certainly has its preservation in mind. Within every unthinking creature, we are informed, there exists a planning, calculating "nature," one that is doubtlessly well equipped with the requisite financial techniques, which conducts its operations on a long-term basis, and about which we shall be shortly hearing some truly amazing things! (SW 1 pp. 566–68)

ON THE MANIFOLD VARIETIES OF LOVE. In the case of
just one major prompting of a drive impulse, the sentiment of love, we must demonstrate that it is not restricted to the exclusive love of one person for another.

In the first place, every person loves everything that he is capable of loving in a constantly changing manner during each of the first four seven-year stages of his life, whereupon, after a long period of growing equability, and with the gradual diminishing of sexual drive activity, a significant alteration again takes place, which is finally succeeded, during the more or less non-sexual phase, by a further transformation of the love impulse. Moreover, everyone experiences love in a different way during each period of his life, for he loves with a love that is appropriate to each father, mother, brother, sister, comrade, friend, superior, subordinate, fellow-worker, public figure, ruler, fellow countrymen, son, daughter, wife, lover, etc.; and with even greater differences, he will love things that are already tinged with love (e.g., memories); and utterly different will be his love for animals, plants, districts (like mountains, heath, sea, etc.), home, youth and so on, not to mention completely intangible love-objects such as career, science, art, religion, motherland, etc. But even within the specifically sex-colored drives, one and the same person in one and the same period of life is faced with a wealth of possible modes of loving which are seemingly inexhaustible. For apart from the fact that, due to the abundance of drive formations, this person is capable of alternately experiencing widely divergent processes as sources of sensual pleasure (the usual combinations: touching and feeling, facial perceptions of the most varied types, acts such as acts of suffering or of torment which the person inflicts or to which he submits), the love which this person bears for one person will differ in kind from the love he bears for another just as surely as the images of the two persons, which inspire that love, differ from each other. (SW 1 pp. 578 ff.)

GOETHE AND THE ROMANTICS. A living totality stands behind both: in Goethe it is Apollo, the god of individuation and, therefore, the god of materialization; in the Romantics, on the other hand, it is the dream-image of the Wild Hunter, the transcendent, drunken, reeling shade of *Wotan*…(RR p. 323)

THE RAPE OF MOTHER EARTH. In 1913, I composed (on request) for the celebratory volume of the *Freideutsche Jugend* on the occasion of the Centenary Festival on the Meissner Heights the address entitled "*Mensch und Erde*" ("Man and Earth"),[1] in which, on the basis of a terrible analysis of the rape of nature by humanity in the present day, I sought to prove that man, as the bearer of Spirit, has torn himself apart just as he is tearing apart the planet to which he owes his birth. (SW 2 p. 1537)

COSMIC POLARITIES. The cosmos lives, and everything that lives is polarized; the two poles of life are soul (*psyche*) and body (*soma*). Wherever there is a living body, there also do we find a soul; wherever there is a soul, there also do we find a living body. The soul is the meaning of the living body, and the image of the body is the phenomenal manifestation of the soul. Whatever appears has a meaning; and every meaning reveals itself in the appearance. The meaning is experienced internally; the appearance is experienced externally. (SW 3 p. 390)

MONISM OF THE SPIRIT. Spirit's essentially monotheistic tendency motivates those scholars who seem to be compelled to subordinate everything that exists to one regnant principle. Spirit aims at universal rule: it unites the world under the *ego* or under the *logos*. When Spirit attained to hegemony, it introduced two novelties: the belief in *historical progress* on the one side, and *religious fanaticism* on the other. The Spirit utilizes force to eliminate all possible rivals. Over the warring and agitated primordial forces, Spirit erected the tyranny of the formula: for some it announces itself as the "ethical autonomy of the individual"; the Catholic Church, on the other hand, still relies on the idea of *holiness*. (RR p. 306)

THE PATH OF SPIRIT. Were we to comprehend everything that impinges on our senses, the world would henceforth be devoid of riddles.

---

1 Available in Ludwig Klages, *The Biocentric Worldview* (London: Arktos, 2013).

That, however, is the path of Spirit: the world of the senses is to be minted into the coin of concepts. (RR p. 466)

THE INVADER. The history of mankind shows that there occurs within man — and only within him — a war to the knife between the power of all-embracing love and a power from outside the spatio-temporal universe; this power severs the poles of life and destroys their unity by "de-souling" the body and disembodying the soul: this power is Spirit (*logos, pneuma, nous*). (SW 3 p. 390)

THE ADVERSARIES. Life and Spirit are two completely primordial and essentially opposed powers, which can be reduced neither to each other, nor to any third term. (SW 2 p. 1527)

BODY AND SOUL. One thesis has guided all of our enquiries for the past three decades or so: that body and soul are inseparably connected poles of the unity of life into which the Spirit inserts itself from the outside like a wedge, in an effort to set them apart from each other; that is, to de-soul the body and disembody the soul, and so, finally, to smother any life that this unity can attain. (SW 1 p. 7)

ON ECSTASY. It is not man's Spirit but his *soul* that is liberated in ecstasy; and his soul is liberated not from his body but from his *Spirit*. (SW 3 p. 390)

ON MATERNAL LOVE. The selfless maternal love of one woman resembles that of another woman to the point of confusion. Since every instinct has something of the "animal" soul in it, maternal love possesses a depth of soul; however, in no way does it have a depth of *Spirit*. Maternal love belongs equally to the animal mother and to the human mother. (SW 3 p. 367)

THE RHYTHM OF LIFE. Whereas every non-human organism pulsates in accord with the rhythms of cosmic life, the law of Spirit has

ordained man's exile from that life. What appears to man, as bearer of
ego-consciousness, in the light of the superiority of calculating thought
above all else, appears to the metaphysician, if he has pondered the matter deeply enough, in the light of an enslavement of life to the yoke of
concepts! (SW 3 p. 391)

ON LIFE AND SPIRIT. Spirit and object are the halves of being; life
and image the poles of actuality—

Spirit "is"; life elapses—

Spirit judges; life experiences—

Judgment is an act; experience is a *pathos*—

Spirit comprehends what exists; life experiences what comes to be—

(Pure) being is outside space and time, and so too is the Spirit; what
comes to be is within space and time, and so too is life—

Being is fundamentally thinkable, but it can never be immediately
experienced; what comes to be can be fundamentally experienced, but it
can never be immediately comprehended—

The act of judgment requires experiencing life, upon which it bases
itself; life does not need the Spirit in order to experience—

Spirit, as that which inheres in life, signifies a force that is directed
against life; life, insofar as it becomes the bearer of Spirit, resists it with an
instinct of defense—

The essence of the historical process of humanity (also called "progress") is the victoriously advancing struggle of the Spirit against life, with
the logically predictable end in the annihilation of the latter. (SW 1 p. 68)

KNOWLEDGE AND POETRY. A deep abyss separates knowledge
and poetry. That which we have *conceived,* can nevermore be *lived.* This
fact accounts for the "unwisdom" of poets. (RR p. 302)

BLONDENESS. The blonde man: man of the abyss, man of the night.
(RR p. 315)

STAGES OF HUMAN DEVELOPMENT. Animal man lives on his instincts, unconsciously; magical man lives in a world of mythic images; spiritual man lives to spout moralistic platitudes. (RR p. 314)

ON THE SEXUAL DRIVE. It is a fundamental and willful falsification to call the sexual drive a drive to *reproduction.* Reproduction is only a potential outcome of sexual intercourse, but it is certainly not included in the actual experience of sexual excitement. The animal knows nothing of it; only man knows. (SW 3 p. 371)

ON THE UNREALITY OF THE FUTURE. Space and time, coexisting in a polar relationship, have this in common: each is extended between the poles of the near and the far. Just as nearness is only *one* regardless of where I stand; and just as, on the other hand, distance [i.e., the "far"] is only *one,* regardless of whether I look to the east, west, north, or south; in the identical sense there can exist only one distance in time relative to one and the same nearness in time. Were there two — i.e., in addition to the distance of the past, a distance into the future — then the nature of the distance to a future point of relationship must necessarily contradict the nature of the distance to a past point. However, since the opposite is the case, the alleged duality of temporal distance constitutes an illusion!

We now explain why we do, in fact, regard the future as a mere illusion. When I contemplate the past, I recollect a reality that once existed; when, on the other hand, I think of the future, I am necessarily thinking of something that is unreal, something that exists solely in this act of thinking. Were all thinking beings to vanish, the past — as it really existed — would remain an unalterable reality; whereas the name "future" would be utterly devoid of meaning in a world wherein there were no beings alive to "think" it. (SW 3 p. 433)

BLOOD AND NERVES. The blood is the site of orgiastic life. What separates the ecstatic nature from the rational is not a refinement of the brain, but a condition of the *blood:* purple blood, blue blood, divine blood. Life resides in blood and pulse. (RR p. 246)

SEEKING AND FINDING. He who seeks shall find, but only after he has surrendered his being to the guidance of the gods. (RR p. 253)

LOGIC AND MYSTICISM. Logic is organized darkness. Mysticism is rhythmic light. (RR p. 253)

MAN AND HOMELAND. The man of instinct is devoted to his homeland. In this feeling for the homeland is rooted all art, nobility, and race. Only the man without a homeland can break with his past. The noble man attaches himself completely to the historical fortunes of his tribe. He will never repudiate his youth; he will never abandon his *home.* (RR p. 246)

MANKIND AND RACE. We must draw a sharp distinction between the man who sees the world as divided between the "human" and the "non-human," and the man who is most profoundly struck by the obvious *racial* groupings of mankind (Nietzsche's "masters"). The bridge that connects us to the Cosmos does not originate in "man," but in *race.* (RR p. 245)

ON LITERARY "CRITICS" AND THE *BILDUNGSPHILISTER.* We are assured that the latest concoction by some school teacher or literary hack is the finest work of the last decade, or even since the death of Nietzsche. A new novel is hailed as the most astounding book ever written on the subject of love. We are told that a recent play has inaugurated a whole new epoch in the art of the theater. We find nothing extraordinary in the claim that some current offering puts Homer, Aeschylus, Pindar, Dante, and Shakespeare quite in the shade; that it inaugurates a completely original school of creative writing; and that the masterpiece under discussion makes all of the efforts of earlier geniuses seem faded and colorless by comparison. Of course, most of our book-reviewers have been well trained in American advertising techniques, and, as a result, their critical reviews have all the subtlety and depth of the blurbs in a publisher's catalogue.

And how readily our educated philistines have rejoiced at this grim state of affairs! (SW 2 p. 1543)

SIN AND THE PAGAN WORLD. The idea of "sin" was quite alien to the pagan world. The ancient pagans knew the gods' hatred as well as their revenge, but they never heard of *punishment* for "sin." The ancient philosophers did understand something of the "good," but when they employed this expression, they were certainly not endorsing the concept of the "sinless." Quite the contrary: they were actually speaking of the pursuit of every type of *excellence.* (RR p. 317)

HERACLITUS. Heraclitus regards the flame as the symbol of actuality; thus, we realize that his soul was *ecstatic.* But he is also the representative of a *rupture,* and this realization enables us to perceive his affinity with ourselves. He was not truly a magician, nor was he a prophet or poet, but, rather: *a dithyrambic thinker.* There exists an insurmountable law that tells us that whatever evokes the greatest *activity* in our inner life is accompanied by the greatest *affectivity:* Heraclitus embodies the philosophical style that maintains a rhythmical mobility; therefore, he is more alert to the centrifugal movement of the flame, and to its hostility to the watery element, than he is to its pulsating incandescence. In a one-sided manner, he misinterprets the sea itself, its breaking waves, and the consummate rush of the maenads...The true fulfillment of the Heraclitean synthesis would be: *a flame-stricken sea.* (RR p. 314)

COSMIC AGGREGATIONS. The cosmic powers do not arrive as drizzling rain. They are rather a torrent, but one can choke that torrent with alien hordes. The torrent will be split up, like molten metal, into a thousand whirling pearls. The cosmic substance remains intact within scattered seeds of noble blood. (RR p. 254)

THE DEATH OF PAGANISM. Every collapse of cosmic creativity is brought about solely by two agencies: *infection from without,* and *weakness from within.* (RR p. 256)

EFFECTS OF CHRISTIANITY. It was Christianity's great achievement to exhaust the soul by defaming sexual passion. But in prohibiting the urge — the "rune within the flesh" (Alfred Schuler) — it thwarted the very possibility of its renewal. And erotic satisfaction is the pre-condition for all cosmic radiance. (RR p. 243)

LIFE AND BEING. All human existence is connected somehow with life: this is so even when life is *degenerating* (as in a polluted race) and when it is *parasitic* (as in the Jew behind his mask). (RR p. 289)

THE TRUE MASTER OF SECRET SOCIETIES. In the forefront of our secret societies, we have the Rosicrucians, the Illuminati, the Freemasons, the "Odd Fellows," and B'nai B'rith. The educated classes are provided with such recent varieties as…the Einstein cult and Freudianism. For half-educated fools we have H. P. Blavatsky, Anny Besant, Rudolf Steiner, and Krishnamurti. For the poor in Spirit, there's the Christian Science of Mrs. Eddy, the Oxford Movement, and biblical fundamentalism. All of these groups, along with innumerable lesser organizations, are humanitarianism's masks. *Jewry is the center from which they are ruled.* (LK GL p. 1345)

ON CHRISTIAN PHILOSOPHY. The values endorsed by Christian philosophical systems are either ethical or logical, i.e., *functional* values devoid of living substance. With that one statement, however, we have *judged* Christian philosophy. (RR p. 300)

CHRIST AND DIONYSOS. Dionysus is the *releasing* god: Eleusis, Lysios. In him the spheres expropriate themselves through commingling. Death in him is eternal rebirth and the meaning of life. Here every tension releases itself and all opposites coalesce. Dionysus is the symbol of the whirlpool; he is chaos as it glowingly gives birth to the world.

In the ego-god, however, we find only an oppressive "truth," an emphasis on purpose (Socrates), and a "beauty of soul" that negates the beauty of the body (mortification of the flesh). Just as one rightly calls Dionysus the releaser, so should Jesus Christ be called the *represser,* because repression is the limiting power that enabled him to conquer so many nations, just as he will, perhaps, eventually conquer all. What Alfred Schuler called his "eagerness for love," can only repress; it can never release. The paradox here is that Jesus insists that he alone is the "redeemer," i.e., the one who releases! (RR p. 267)

THE CHRISTIAN SICKNESS. From the universal love of the wandering Germanic tribes, Christianity fashioned the insanity known as *redemption.* (RR p. 250)

CHRISTIANITY AND WAKEFULNESS. Even in the garden of olives Christ begged his disciples to remain awake by his side. The saints indicate by their sleeplessness that nothing can harm them. Christianity is the war against sleep and dream, two states for which a reviving elemental life will always be yearning. Against the activity of astral wakefulness, elemental life places consummation and the pagan feeling for fate. True pagans regard sleeplessness as the most monstrous conceivable evil. In addition, the wakefulness of the Christian manifests a slavish impulse: the lurking wariness and prudence of submissive souls. (RR p. 253)

FROM A LETTER RE: "ANTI-SEMITISM." I've never endorsed the claim that the Nazi Bonzes belonged to a superior race. However, I must also add that I have consistently refused to accept the claim of a certain other race to be the "chosen people." The arrogance is identical in both cases, but with this significant distinction: after waging war against mankind for more than three thousand years, Jewry has finally achieved total victory over all of the nations of the earth.

Therefore, I will have nothing to do with the contemporary kowtow-ing on the part of almost the entire civilized world before the haters of all mankind (Tacitus spoke of Christians, but he certainly meant the Jews, as will be obvious to every alert reader of his works). I despise all this kow-towing to the Jews as an utterly mendacious tactical ploy. (LK GL p. 1350)

THE PROPHECY OF A JEWISH FRIEND. I might easily fill

ten pages...with anecdotes concerning the life of Richard Perls. He was born a Jew, but he eventually abandoned Judaism, a religion that he had come to hate. One year before his death, which occurred, to the best of my recollection, in 1897, he said to me: "Herr Klages, the ancient world was destroyed by Judaism, just as the modern world is about to be!" When I voiced my skepticism as to the accuracy of his prophecy...he merely responded: "Just wait — you will live to see my prophecy fulfilled!" (LK GL p. 196)

PAGANISM AND CHRISTIANITY. Life is instantaneous, death

is duration: this truth must stand above the threshold of our paganism. With this truth we inaugurate the depreciation of Spirit... (RR p. 260)

CHRISTIAN AND PAGAN. A pagan can become a Christian in his

old age: the living substance disintegrates, and the rotting residue is barely functional. On the other hand, never will a Christian become a pagan. (RR p. 264)

CHRISTIANITY AND SELF-PRESERVATION. Christianity aimed

at the preservation of the individual ego, in whose service it preaches "compassion." Christian compassion is hostile to life, because the laws of life are not the laws of the ego: therefore, Nietzsche was correct in spurn-ing it. The paganism that he wished to proclaim, on the other hand, was a splendid surrender of the ego and, hence, a phenomenon of life.

Christian compassion, however, took on a more sympathetic form within the Nordic world, where compassion was felt towards even the animals and plants.

In addition, there is still another type: *cosmic* compassion (the erotic), which is a positive stirring of life and affection that we should never discourage. (RR p. 301)

CHRISTIANITY AND TIME. Christianity first changed time into the historical "once and once only." (RR p. 303)

THE GREAT DECEIVER. To the Jew, everything human is a sham. One might even say that the Jewish face is nothing but a *mask*. The Jew is not a liar: *he is the lie itself.* From this vantage point, we can say that the Jew is not a man...He lives the pseudo-life of a ghoul whose fortunes are linked to Yahweh-Moloch. He employs deception as the weapon with which he will exterminate mankind. The Jew is the very incarnation of the unearthly power of destruction. (RR p. 330)

HOW YAHWEH EXPRESSES HIMSELF. Yahweh's medium of expression is the *gesture*. The meaning of all of his gestures, so far as they actually possess any metaphysical significance, can be interpreted as an ever-deeper subjugation of one principle at the hands of an ever-loftier one: consecration, blessing, etc., on the one side, and repentance, contrition, and adoration on the other. Semitic religiosity is restricted to adoring worshipper and adored deity. When this religiosity attaches itself solely to the personal, the emblem of worship becomes the individual person. Only the Semitic religions bow to the "One God." In adoration, the believer achieves the non-rational form of ego-consciousness. Pagan rationality glides right past the god to the ego; in the Semitic "service of God," however, the transcendental "One" brings destruction to the world of "appearances." Apollo is, so to speak, an ethically developed Dionysus; he works on the soil of *blood-thinning*. Yahweh is the all-devouring nothingness; he works on the soil of *blood-poisoning*. (RR p. 321)

THE CULT OF THE CHRIST. It is impossible to conceive of a more fatal blindness than that of the cult instigated by this Jewish sectarian and his apostles and camp followers. Torn from the bonds of nature and the past, man must now direct his gaze at the wasteland known as the "future"; into that desert he stares, paralyzed by dread of the vengeful Jew-God. And before this insane masquerade of the "kingdom come," the "last judgment," and "eternal punishment" can be consummated, the true heroes and the real gods must first be made to grovel before the cross! (RR p. 285)

EROS. Eros is elemental or cosmic in so far as the individual who is seized by Eros experiences, as it were, a pulsating, inundating stream of electricity. (RR p. 387)

EROS (AS OPPOSED TO "SEXUALITY"). In the ancient world, Eros was always closely associated with *ethos*. The Christian era inaugurated the reign of "sexuality" and its necessary complement: *asceticism*. Tension and hostility begin to infect intimate relationships, until eventually we arrive at the "war between the sexes."…The Jew consummates the total victory of "sexuality," although, of course, he knows nothing of genuine sensuality, as he is a mere lecher. True Eros is eventually demoted to the status of a mere sexual "stimulant." (RR p. 349)

NOBILITY AND RACE. Nobility belongs exclusively to the man of race. There is no such thing as moral nobility, only a moral *egoism*. The downfall of a master caste is the very essence of tragedy. A sense of honor is inborn in every aristocrat, and the duel is the knightly principle incarnate. Only he who is without race can endure disgrace. The master scorns the very idea of a negotiated settlement. The master perishes from wounded pride. (RR p. 245)

ROME AND GERMANIA. One may be a fixed star or a planet; even as a fixed star one may be a planet, for there are both planetary suns as well as stationary ones. The Roman was the center, the German the periphery, but the German sphere was so distant that, to the Roman, it seemed to be a mere tangent point, an entity struggling on the margins of his world. The Roman sun is not the German's center, for Rome is itself a peripheral creation in the eyes of the German during the time of his colossal wanderings. But then he was given the Cross: now the need for redemption becomes his guiding star, and he is soon at work forging Judea's ring of power. (RR p. 252)

THE DIOSCURI. The Dioscuri of Mankind: the hero and the poet. The first one lives the primordial image; the other perceives and reveals it. They are sons born of the same mother: there is no other metaphysical brotherhood. (RR p. 288)

THE HOMOSEXUAL CHARACTER. Peripheral qualities: lack of conviction, self-flattery. Closer to the center: his personality is more selfish than that of any woman. In general, the homosexual has no sense for facts. Even closer to the center: the most peculiar form of megalomania. He even believes that he understands love, while he sneers at love between man and woman as merely a mask behind which lurks the breeding impulse. He sees himself as the center of the world, a world that he believes would collapse were his own surroundings to collapse. His house, his garden, and his crowd are for him the whole world. He cannot turn his gaze from his favorite playroom, which explains why his horizon is limited to himself and his highly talented associates. Psychologically, his incapacity for abstract thought is consistent with his persistent identification with the feminine character. Alone, he manifests a propensity to confuse his own little world with the real one. Another way of expressing our view: in general, he doesn't believe in the external world at all, but in a world which is part of himself, and, so to speak, his private property. In the presence of his fellow men, the homosexual presents himself as a sort of patron; he wants to be everyone's father, ruler, and general authority-figure; he even values this relationship as a form of erotic satisfaction. Favorite hobbies: boys and Platonism. The salient secondary qualities are: sensitivity, ability to scent a change in the weather, a taste for politics, a knowledge of the ways of men, and an inability to commune directly with nature; he prefers aestheticism, culture, art, poetry, and philosophy. Although he has a predilection for trees, animals, and parks, etc., he has no feeling whatsoever for *elemental* nature. A tentative explanation: his whole being radiates exhaustion and disarray. He always stands on the outside, not in the sense of Judaism, but more in the manner of the paranoiac, who, although having some sort of vitality, has no involvement with the universal stream of life. That is why, in fact, his inability to love leaves him receptive only to what is *loveable* in life. Thus, he experiences every deeper association with another person as just one more variety of self-love, as if he were merely encountering a side of his own personality; he requires these fresh, counterfeit connections with persons and things so that he might enhance his own self-love (the "smugness" of every homosexual). While Jewish exclusiveness leads to life-envy and the drive to *disintegration,* the homosexual is led by a drive to *contraction.* Just as the homosexual carries within him his own little world, his overall horizon presents a closed "circle." He substitutes his finite world for the infinity of the real world. These compulsions once ruled the Rome of the Caesars as they still rule the Rome of the Popes. (RR p. 366)

WORSHIP OF THE STATE. We hope that we need not emphasize that our denunciation of "state-thought" is not in the least an attack "Capitalism" from the standpoint of some variety of "Socialism!" "Capitalism," Liberalism," Marxism," "Communism," etc., are stages on one and the same path to the mechanization of all human associations, a path that leads — as only the blind would fail to see — to a collectivist destination. (AG p. 178)

SUBSTANTIAL THOUGHT. The forbidding of thought on the part of ascetics speaks volumes in favor of thought. The substance of thought possesses the power to embody itself. The experience of thought can even rattle the gates to the empire of the sun, and set the world of images *vibrating.* (RR p. 306)

THE SACRED. Suppose a thinker has convinced himself that the far-famed sanctity of the "three-fold" — the triad of Poseidon, the tripod of the Pythian Oracle, the three divisions of the world of the gods, the Christian Trinity, the Three Norns, and so many other items — is the genuine experience of a three-fold system of *reality*. He will (provided the Orphic Eros itself is a matter of living experience to him) likewise seek behind the three-fold phenomena embodied in theogonic myth an *experienced actuality*. The cosmic *rush*, as the loftiest of all chaotic intoxicants, must thus be understood in its three unique forms. Many years have passed since the author of these lines first drew attention to the three basic modes of the rush, viz., the heroic, the erotic, and the magical…In the magical mode, the rush manifests its nature in a dual connection to the nightly firmament and to the realm of the dead. Its historical high point was reached in the "Magism" of the Medes and in the Egyptian funerary cult. Perhaps its purest conceptual precipitate is to be found in Chaldean astrology. The heroic-tragic rush…was embodied in that epoch of late "Pelasgian" humanity upon which historians have bestowed the title of "the heroic age." Among the four heroic peoples with whom we are familiar, the rush was embodied in the magnificent creations of the epic poets. The most striking characteristic of the epic lies in the fact that here the death of the ego is achieved through the death of the warrior's body in battle. Its most superb manifestation took place in the Germanic world…the doomed warriors experience death in battle as the kiss of the Valkyrie; the hero knew that he would soon awaken from the torment and darkness of destruction — in Valhalla's realm of the dead! (SW 3 p. 398)

WOMAN AND POET. The woman and the poet are close relations. He is the voice of her yearnings. In the wake of the poets moves the procession of the Bacchantes. Poets are the interpreters of Dionysus. (RR p. 262)

AFFECT AND LIFE. Life incorporates the affect; the ego disembodies it. (RR p. 356)

THE WESTERN LIGHT. "What a commotion is caused by light!" This is the western light, the showering bolts of light, the storm of radiance. (RR p. 303)

IDEALISM. Idealism is the poverty of the wealthy and the wealth of the impoverished. (RR p. 304)

PRIMAL IMAGERY OF THE WORLD. Every region of the world can instantaneously become the complete possession of the soul; the region's essential complexion remains the same. In that instant, one gains a glimpse of eternity. (RR p. 244)

ON POSSESSING WEALTH. Many first possess wealth, and are then possessed by it. Many lose their wealth, and, in turn, become the richer for their loss. (RR p. 253)

ON MEMORY. It requires no experiment to prove that a content having meaning is more easily memorized, and is retained for a greater length of time, than, for example, a series of meaningless syllables; and that verse, especially rhymed verse, is more easily retained than prose. Further, we are all aware that repetition facilitated learning. If at one time I have studied physics, and, as I think, have forgotten everything about the subject in the course of time, then if I once more take up the laws of physics, I shall nevertheless learn them much more quickly than when I first studied this subject. Numerous experiments have shown that a distribution of repetitions over several days is more favorable to the process of memorizing than their immediate accumulation. Further, it also appears to be the case that a coherent whole is more effortlessly mastered if it is learned in one piece than if it is divided into parts to be learned in separate pieces: finally, that relatively quick learning is preferable to relatively slow learning. In these respects, at least, all persons are more or less alike, although there are a very few notable instances in absolute speed of learning and the length of retention, under equal conditions, of memorizing. It should also be emphasized that typically quick learners are by no means also quick to forget. Thus, it is certain that some men have a stronger innate memory than others. (SW 4 p. 261)

COUNTERFEIT NARCOTICS. The god of the modern age is "Mammon," and its symbol is money (paper, thus unreal; "capital," thus heartless). Mammon's temple is the Stock Exchange. Slavery and depravity are its servants: both are narcotics, both are counterfeit, both are *perverted.* (RR p. 354)

THE COSMOS AND THE EARTH. Though our yearning presses towards the most distant reaches of the Cosmos, we are nurtured only upon the earth. (RR p. 258)

EROS AND CHAOS. Eros without chaos: humanitarianism. Chaos without Eros: demonic devastation. Eros within chaos: *Dionysus.* (RR p. 265)

PLEASURE IN THE RAIN. In the fall of rain we find the marriage of the telluric and sidereal elements. (RR p. 265)

ELEMENT. The element is the ultimate manifestation of animated being. Perpetually, life drifts towards sleep — the road leading downward; endlessly, it transmits signals of war — the road leading upward. Gaia opens eyelids heavy with slumber to gaze upon the heroes and wizards in the distance. (RR p. 261)

NO EXIT. There can be no liberation through denial, but only through fulfillment. In despair, life is shattered, but this does not lead to a marriage with the Cosmos: the new state would be just as miserable as the old. (RR p. 273)

ROME AND GERMANIA. The Roman surrounded himself with walls, the German with falling rain and wind-blown trees: to them he sings, about them he thinks, and in their midst he dreams his inner dream. (RR p. 277)

FUNCTION OF TIME. In the life that rings us round, time and eternity are identical. Individual life ages, but essential life has the power to rejuvenate itself from within. (RR p. 277)

THE ETERNAL "JUNGFRAU." The summit of the "*Jungfrau*" is the symbol of the eternally fresh dew, the eternal morning, the never-ending and never-aging beginning, the perpetual today, the undiminished, radiant heights of the timeless first moment. (RR p. 281)

MEANING AND PURPOSE. Everything purposeful is meaningless, and everything meaningful is purposeless. (RR p. 280)

A NOTE. The image that falls upon the senses: that, and nothing besides, is the meaning of the world. (RR p. 280)

THE DEED. Only one connection to the future is authentic enough to vindicate the unreality of a "future": the deed that this future summoned into being. Anything else is the wishful thinking of pious fools. (RR p. 280)

HISTORY. History knows no tragedy, but only success and failure. The tragic view of historical events was a misunderstanding hatched by poets. (RR p. 280)

"ASIATISM." Spiritualism is of Asiatic derivation, but there it has two origins: out of the revolt of the slave, and the debauchery of the king. The gruesome mania of domination and the base servility of slavery are both symptoms of the *excess* that is characteristic of the Asiatic nature. (RR p. 302)

THE ORIENT. The ardor of dream. The objective world trembles dubiously in the exaggerated blaze of the noontide desert. The soul respires as if in a brooding pregnancy. Finally, there strides out of the seething, vibrating blue, a mirage: the *Fata Morgana*. (RR p. 243)

APHORISM ON CHINA. China is the land of the deepest wisdom, and all of its wisdom teaches: learn to endure life, have patience! The wisdom of China is unmystical; it divides its attention equally between the soul and the real world. (RR p. 293)

THE OPPOSED WILL. Feelings of loathing are far more characteristic of man than are his preferences. Consciousness begets restraint. (RR p. 301)

POLARITIES. 1. Essential — Cosmic; 2. Telluric — Sidereal; 3. Fixed — Wandering; 4. Cell — Element; 5. Chaos — *Wotan*. (RR p. 318)

THE SUN CHILD. Children of the sun have no history, for no child ever has a history. From the outset, however, the ego does have a history, in the individual as in mankind as a whole: it *ages*. (RR p. 318)

THE "FINGER OF GOD." In the "finger of God" as well as in the stigmata, I see the perversion of the "dactylology" [= "sign language"] of the ancient world. (RR p. 322)

THE ROAD TO DEGENERATION. Love is aborted by contemplation, passion by the deed. Contemplation degenerates into science, the deed into theatrics. (RR p. 342)

"MONISM." Every form of so-called "Monism" confuses unity and connection. It runs aground on such crucial concepts as extension, space, and time. (RR p. 362)

DESTINY AND MEMORY. That which inspires the deepest desire in us, arises through the medium of our darker childhood memories. (RR p. 474)

FLUX AND MOVEMENT. The flux is the image of the happening; the movement is its visible form. (RR p. 360)

LIFE AND FLUX. Life is flux, permanence is death. Life as endurance culminates in the faith in the actuality of *things,* in the madness of *duration.* The Cosmos incarnates the actuality of an unceasing process. Only in the interplay of fixed and wandering powers lies the guarantee of life. (RR p. 249)

THE CLOVEN SUBSTANCE. The soul is divided by border regions. Love becomes yearning. Rejected by the Cosmos, blundering mankind goes astray. (RR p. 251)

PAGAN LOVE. Only love delivers us from the labyrinth of the world. Only love releases the individual to cosmic life. Cosmic man experiences nothing human other than his love, and his love incarnates his melancholy-joyous revelry. (RR p. 255)

EVOLUTION OF THE IMAGE. The primordial whirlpool deposits images in the blood. These images *will* themselves into visibility. The awakened man forges the images out of rock and ore. Dream-dark knowledge shackles them with decree and edict. Cosmic Eros lives within a molten ring of imagery. (RR p. 254)

WILLFULNESS. Willfulness knows no end. It is the spawn of want and need. It is an empty belly that gobbles up the Cosmos. "You must will," says every moralist from Socrates to Kant... (RR p. 258)

SOUL AND INDIVIDUAL. In the soul, the individual is not truly an individual, but a cosmic wave. The soul is able to bypass its bodily-spiritual uniqueness, to go beyond, to become a whirlpool of universal life. Within the blood of those who are rich in soul-substance, atoms of fire circulate: the pores, the mouth, and the sexual organs are the portals of life. (RR p. 263)

ROMAN AND BARBARIAN. Only the barbarians (Germans, Muslims, and Tatars), and not the men of classical antiquity, understood the *rush of battle*. When the Greek or Roman warrior met the barbarian on the field of battle, astuteness conquered the rush. (RR p. 317)

CONCEPT, NAME, THING. The origin of thought is not to be found in the duality: concept and thing, but in the trinity: concept, name, and thing. The name embraces the totality, but concept and thing are its poles. This enables us to clarify the magical effect that the word can have upon a consciousness that is receptive to the symbol. (RR p. 361)

DISCOVERY AND OBSERVATION. We do not make discoveries through observation; we only *confirm* them. (RR p. 362)

RHYTHM AND MEASURE. The entire phenomenal universe is organized upon a rhythmic basis. Science has correctly discovered — although it has had some difficulty in comprehending its discovery — that sound, heat, and electricity all have a rhythmical nature. (SW 7 p. 329)

SONG AND RHYTHM. Every song has its rhythm and its measure. Perhaps, it was only by means of the erroneous identification of rhythm and measure, that it became possible strictly to separate them. Although rhythm and measure may seem to be as intimately intertwined as a pair of dancers, they are, by nature and by origin, not mere opposites, but opposites striving against each other; in all of nature only man has thought to make one substance of rhythm and nature, and in this attempt he has had to use *force*. (SW 7 p. 330)

ANIMALS AND RHYTHM. The flapping of a bird's wings in flight is rhythmical, as is the wild horse's stamping, and the gliding of the fish through the water. However, animals cannot run, fly, or swim according to measure; nor can man himself breathe according to measure. (SW 7 p. 336)

LIFE AND SELF-PRESERVATION. The laws of life are not the laws of self-preservation. This is the dreadful side of life, and it serves as the basis of all tragedy. (RR p. 246)

BEAUTY AND EGO. Neither the ego nor its deeds are beautiful. Man is beautiful only to the extent that he participates in the eternal soul of the Cosmos. Beauty is always demonic, and the proper objects of our adoration are the *gods*. (RR p. 246)

WORK AND WONDER. Deed, work, and system belong to the realm of Spirit. What cannot be wonder will become work. Unconsciously, the maternal ground of the soul generates the shining purple blood; the imagistic force, however, is masculine, sunny, *spiritual*. (RR p. 256)

FESTIVALS. Every festival will be a play between distances. (RR. p. 269)

VIEWPOINTS.

1. *The logocentric ascetic.* His view emerges from one point and directs itself to one point. He discovers neither the colors within him nor the things without. He sees only radiating points.

2. *The cellular-microcosmic man.* He sees within him the colors of plants and animals, or he sees columns, screens, and hanging lamps. He celebrates his festival in the purple vaults of his soul.

3. *Macrocosmic-heroic man.* He is utterly outside himself, in rain, burning sun, forest, ocean, and open country. He knows no self-consciousness. He experiences the signals of heroic battles, whilst his gaze dreams with the sapling in the fireplace. His dream-laden view is analogous to physical blindness. Indeed, Homer *is* blind.

4. *Teleological man.* His view emerges from out of the ego, and is directed straight back at the ego. He never contemplates; he merely *observes*. (RR p. 305)

CREATION AND POLITICS. Politicians compulsively spread the news that they are making sacrifices every minute of the day; this is, of course, the most idiotic type of verbal pomposity. We can identify here the frightful egomania of our politicians and their deficient spirit of sacrifice. Behind all of the turgid tirades of our politicians there lurks an utter lack of principle.

Why should one use the word "cultured" when speaking of those who, in lieu of courage or soul, have matching volumes of memoirs brewing in their bellies? (RR p. 307)

THE DREAMER. Eros holds absolute sway only within a magical actuality. The world-image passes through the magical stage to the second condition of consciousness, one that is no longer disturbed by experiences of "near" and "far." Already, the dream-laden Eros is becoming a weaker Eros. In moralistic civilizations, cosmic man tears himself away from an actuality that has become commonplace. Because he has "received a shock" in contact with this tiresome reality, he becomes a "dreamer." We are closer to things than were the Romantics, which may account for the fact that our sorrow has a more acrid savor. (RR p. 311)

THE MEANING OF "RATIO." In *ratio*, life is a synonym for calculation. God is the greatest *number*…Time realizes its potential on the *line* of progress. Yahweh, the "devouring flame," *cancels* out the moment. God is a mere word, a predicate without a subject. (RR p. 275)

TWO PRIMORDIAL SPIRITS. There is a gloom that shines on the outside, and there is an inner light that sheds an outer darkness. That one brightens and redeems, but is itself blind; this one sees and understands, but sheds no light. That one comprehends a world without understanding himself; this one comprehends himself, without understanding the world. (RR p. 285)

TWO DISCOVERERS. The thoughtful: he cannot leave his place, although he has the walking stick that reaches into every distance. The farseeing: he has no walking stick, and yet he wanders. (RR p. 285)

MAN AND DEATH. In all of creation only man lives in opposition to death. Although the doctrines of every mystagogue aim at stripping death of its power, they all go utterly astray: instead of encompassing the downfall of the ego, they encourage the belief in the prolongation of the ego's existence into infinity. (RR p. 287)

WISDOM OF LIFE. What befalls every man is that which belongs to him, and we can only lose that which we no longer possess. (RR p. 287)

ON THE PRIMORDIAL WORD. In the primordial word, showing and working co-exist. The wave of the Cosmos reaches its highest crest when it displays the soul in the garb of the word. (RR p. 287)

ON BEAUTY. Beauty is but the cloak of happiness. Where joy tarries, there also is beauty; however, beauty itself may become ugly in our moments of repugnance. (RR p. 468)

MAN AND WOMAN. Woman lives more in being, man more in consciousness. To woman belongs the present, to man the future or the past.

Masculine logic corresponds to woman's feeling for measure.

Man strives, but woman lives.

Man is centrifugal force, but woman is weightier.

Woman is short-sighted regarding the "far," man regarding the "near."

Man always sees aims and, thus, the abstractions at hand; woman first teaches him the joy in the real world. (RR p. 468)

INVULNERABLE. At the summit of his vitality, man is invulnerable. In the moments of our greatest certainty of being, we are stronger than external destiny. No one and nothing can slay us. (RR p. 473)

KNOWLEDGE AND PROOF. The most essential knowledge is not susceptible to proof. (RR p. 474)

SHADOW. You shoot up like the shadow of a body that flees before the light. (RR p. 463)

SOUL OF THE WORLD. Whenever we destroy something, we destroy along with it part of the soul of the world. (RR p. 462)

GRIEF. Grief drags his dread through the Cosmos. (RR p. 436)

ON THE POET. One misleads oneself regarding the poet if one sees the essence of his art in depth of feeling and passion. Whoever finds inside himself a spark of the poetic Spirit can only become a true poet if that which has moved his soul since the days of his youth is the *word,* the word as expression of the connection between his soul and the images of the world. (RR p. 472)

ROOTS IN THE PAST. The roots of my nature reach into antediluvian pre-history. There exists within me a sympathy with the most distant past, with the longest vanished stages of development, with the primitive basalt, with the oceans, clouds and storms. (RR p. 472)

FEELINGS AND SPEECH. When our feelings were most intense, our speech was still constrained and bound. Now, as we think of more audacious words, the waves of feeling have already receded. (RR p. 472)

TEARS FOR THE DEAD. We believe that we weep for the dead; in truth, we only pity ourselves for being eternally separated from the deceased. (RR p. 462)

FORMULA FOR THE ETHOS OF CHARACTER. The egoist: I will. The altruist: I shall. The sentimentalist: you will. The ascetic: he wills (I must). Animal man: it wills (I must). Elemental man: it happens (I must). (RR p. 481)

LIFE AND PHILOSOPHY. To pour life into concepts at a venture: that is the mission of philosophy. (RR p. 478)

SENTIMENTALITY. Sentimentality is the yearning for images on the part of those who are unfit to behold them. (RR p. 475)

THE RECLUSE AND THE ACTIVE MAN. Were we to resign all [social] intercourse with mankind, we may become mystics, pedants, or hair-splitting metaphysicians, but we could never become masters of characterology; and the danger of self-deception to such a recluse may become enormous. The famous *tat tvam asi* does perhaps strike some prophetic chord or other; but only weary souls' love of solitude could help to spread a saying whose delusive profundity conceals the fact that the world is immeasurably greater, richer, and more manifold that that part of it which fits into a single impoverished formula. Qualities that are to enter into our consciousness must receive their daily exercise; and the most important are only exercised among our fellow men. A man may have a greater capacity for jealousy than most, and yet he might never have the slightest awareness of this fact until day when he falls violently in love. Many inhabitants of the big city overestimate their physical courage, because city life rarely gives occasion for serious tests of courage. Goethe never tired of insisting that only the "active" man can accurately estimate his strengths and weaknesses. (SW 4 p. 212)

MACROBIOTICS. The loftiest morality of macrobiotics: be courageous, serene, and cautious. The only problem is: either one already possesses these three qualities, or one can never possess them. (RR p. 456)

UNDERSTANDING AND WILL. Understanding is the emergence of Spirit out of itself; the will represents its return into itself. In its conceptual, rational, explanatory mode, Spirit loses itself in the world, is "just" to the images, and, thus, is centrifugal. In its volitional mode, on the other hand, Spirit takes the world into itself as if it were plunder and, thus, Spirit is centripetal. One can refute proofs, but not *purposes*. (RR p. 362)

THINKING AND BREATHING. In the proper sense, thinking is volitional; thinking, however, is an interior *speaking*. Therefore, excessive thought leads to shallow respiration and shortness of breath. This is especially true of emotional thinking: it *takes one's breath away.* (RR p. 353)

PLAGIARISM. There may indeed be more profound thinkers among my contemporaries, as well as more learned and more successful ones; but in one area I have certainly achieved the world-record: I am the most *plundered* author on the contemporary scene. (SW 2 p. 1535)

DEAD THINGS. That which has been pierced by the searchlight of the intellect is instantaneously transformed into a mere *thing,* a quantifiable object for our thought that is henceforth only mechanically related to other objects. The paradoxical expression of a modern sage, "we perceive only that which is dead," is a lapidary formulation of a deep truth. (SW 3 p. 652)

ON NORMATIVE ETHICS. From Socrates through Kant and into the present, the command is reiterated, in the hundreds of refractions and metamorphoses that constitute every normative system of ethics, that man's task is to "control himself," to subjugate his desires to the rule of reason, to moderate his feelings, if not to extirpate them entirely. (SW 4 p. 552)

THE EGOIST. His formula is not the "will-to-power," but the *noli turbare* ["do not disturb me"] of Archimedes. The sympathetic feelings in the egoist are inverted, and they assume the morally colored drives: to accumulate "honors," to hate, and to envy. He possesses a thoroughly "cold" nature, inclines to solitude, and chooses only such occupations as will permit him to remain alone within himself. He is inartistic, his soul is devoid of the feminine element, he will never attract disciples, and he always chooses himself as his favorite field of contemplation. (SW 4 p. 5)

KNOWLEDGE AND ACTUALITY. The knowledge of life is not life, just as the knowledge of death is not death itself. (RR p. 280)

ON LANGUAGE AND VISION. Among older students of language, Lazarus Geiger, in his book on the *Origins and Development of Human Language and Reason* (1868), which, unfortunately, remained a sort of "torso," held the view (which is correct in fact, though badly worked out by him and, until today, unappreciated) that the development of language, as well as the development of all human thought, takes place under the overwhelming influence of the sense of sight. Now, if it be granted that, for reasons connected with the theory of consciousness, we held this assertion to be correct, we will certainly not reject the confirmation of this position that the testimony of language provides in the following cases, which are merely a few among many. The German "*Wissen*" (to know) leads us back to the Indo-European root *wid,* which in almost all of the Indo-European languages means interchangeably "to find," "to cognize," or "to see": Sanskrit *vid* = "to find"; Latin *videre* = "to see"; and Gothic *witan* = "to observe." Thus, in German the chief words for the most crucial functions and results of the intellect are taken from the sphere of sight: view, insight, intuition, and also aim. On the other hand, the development of the Latin *cernere* passes from "to sever" through the abstraction "to distinguish" to "perceive with the eyes" and to "see a thing clearly." Such examples, which can easily be multiplied, shed light on the inner connection that connects the power of judgment and that of sight: that is, of course, according to the "spirit of language." (SW 4 pp. 234–5)

FORMULA AND MEANING. Characterological terminology must do justice to the present meaning of words and not to that of some past era; nevertheless, it will do its part to prevent the mechanization of terms of speech that once were important, and to maintain intact the best part of its original content in a more rigid framework. "While the formulae remain, the meanings may at any time revive," says John Stuart Mill in his magnificent chapter in the *System of Logic* on the pre-requisites of a philosophical language. "To common minds only that portion of the meaning is in each generation suggested of which that generation possesses the counterpart in its own habitual experience. But the words and propositions are ready to suggest to any mind duly prepared the remainder of the meaning." This pronouncement outlines a plan, the execution of which would constitute the achievement of a comprehensive characterology. (SW 4 p. 236)

ON THE DELUSION OF "PROGRESS." The greatest sage living ten thousand years ago, and who passed through all of the earth's prehistoric tribes, could not have calculated that after so many centuries or millennia the historical process would be initiated in one or another of them. In fact, no sage of classical antiquity predicted the Christian process, which had, in fact, already commenced with Socrates. If we were acquainted with Western man only, then, however profoundly we examined the conflict of Spirit and soul within him, we could never derive the Indian species of the same conflict, still less its manifestations in the cultures of the Far East; for, without experience, we could not be acquainted with the vitality of the Far East. Those who imagine that the study of the customs and especially the history of mankind enables them to predict a series of concrete manifestations, should foretell for our benefit what would be the appearance of buildings, costumes, and languages three thousand years into the future; or let them predict the direction of change of these and other crystallizations of human nature just thirty years ahead. If they cannot do these things, or if they consistently miss the mark, let them confess to themselves at least that, misled by erroneous and shoddy notions spawned by a delusive belief in "progress," they have undertaken an impossible task. For we know of no "progress" other than that which results in complete dissolution and final destruction, in so far as things continue on the straight course down which "civilized" humanity has been racing since 1789 at an ever-accelerating pace. Likewise, we know nothing of the capacity of life to generate new formations, nor do we understand life's "emergency reserves." We know of no clearer manner of formulating this view than by borrowing the phraseology of science, and stating that it is necessary to become acquainted biologically with the notion that at certain stages of a living series new forces emerge whose development cannot be forecast from previous forms. (SW 4 pp. 238–9)

On Resistance to Expression. Every animal, and man in particular, has an interest in *not* revealing certain mental processes. A man in love seeks to conceal that love in public, a shy man his shyness, an ambitious man his ambition, an envious man his envy, a jealous man his jealousy, etc. Many will do more than hide their true inclination, and they will seek to simulate the opposite, as we all do a thousand times semi-automatically when we treat a person, towards whom our sentiments are anything but friendly, with conventional acts of courtesy. Originally, all self-control served as self-protection. Now if we consider that man has been forced during innumerable centuries to practice self-control in order to preserve his life and well-being intact, we would be forced to consider it to be a miracle if no organic resistance to expression had arisen within him.

We can discover countless prototypes of this resistance in the animal world. When many animals feign death if they imagine themselves to be in danger, this is no action, but a reaction that occurs necessarily, and which is rooted in the instinct for self-preservation; and it takes place at the expense of the fear that without a doubt possesses the animal and which might otherwise result in flight. But the technique of deception and the drill in maintaining a countenance received an intensification far beyond all such cases in the animal kingdom from the fact that man's communal mode of living by prehistoric times had come under the dominion of cultic customs whose sphere of influence, diminishing progressively in historic epochs, was replaced by no milder set of ethical commands. An infraction of customs, and, at a later time, an infraction of ethical rules and a sense of right, resulted at the least in temporary or permanent exile from the community, and hence, among primitive peoples, in almost certain destruction; among civilized peoples, such an infraction would result in an ostracism that in extreme cases seems to have been hardly less fearful; to say nothing of the bloody side of criminal justice, which transcends any notion that an individual may have formed of hell itself. If it could be determined with dynamometrical precision whether men fear more the loss of life or the loss of reputation, we might discover quite a few slaves of their honor, who would be ready, if necessary, to risk their lives in order to preserve it. Many soldiers have found the courage required to face a storm of bullets only through the dread of being tainted by an imputation of cowardice.

We arrive at the root of the matter when we consider that the need for self-esteem, which is omnipotent in man, was necessarily fused with the demands of the community. Thus, from prehistoric times, man cultivated his peculiar sense of honor, which fundamentally distinguishes him from the rest of the animal kingdom. (SW 4 pp. 315–6)

NATURE OF CONSCIOUSNESS I. Death only attains to being as the correlative of life. Where there is no contemplation, there can be no distinguishing between the living and the dead. (RR p. 299)

NATURE OF CONSCIOUSNESS II. Destiny is never housed within the individual; high above the tragedy of the past stands the poet and his deeper necessity. Every philosophy that holds the individual's suffering as the weightiest matter, that recognizes the overriding importance of purposes and aims, is merely *physics;* such a philosophy is not admitted to the forecourt of true understanding. Thought and transient existence are inferior things, shadows of actualities. But whence the shadow and whence the slag of the primeval fire? What is the meaning and origin of our conceptual consciousness? (RR p. 247)

NATURE OF CONSCIOUSNESS III. The real presences in the soul are not feelings, but *images.* Feelings are attendant phenomena of the coming to consciousness of psychical processes that become more weighty as matter attains to independent existence. Consciousness recognizes no qualitative distinction between the simplest act of observation and the strongest affect. On the contrary, the sober soul can manifest itself in the simplest display. So it was for the "childhood"-phase of Spirit; with the maturation of Spirit, it is no longer the case. We err when we ascribe the feeling of the "rush" to the Mycenaean epoch. Homer knew it not, and even in our fairy tales we find ourselves witnessing the violation of the soul. Those who *must* break through the defensive bastions of consciousness in order to renew the powers of life, will experience the authentic immersion in the force of the *rush*. (RR p. 247)

NATURE OF CONSCIOUSNESS IV. A platitude holds that ignorance increases as one accumulates possessions. Nevertheless, all thought occurs as *restraint.* For this reason, negative decisions — as in matters of taste — are more significant than the positive ones. Whatever our mouths shout most loudly will unfailingly be found to occupy the smallest area of our inner world. The "idea" represents *stress,* and not the Heraclitean flux. The man who summons the troops to battle is seldom a warrior, for orators tend to avoid combat. Within the true expert, there flows an unconscious stream of life; within the intellectual, on the other hand, one finds only pipe-dreams and *ideas.* (RR p. 301)

BODY AND SOUL. To "de-body" and to "de-soul" are one and the same thing. The body *is* the soul, or at the very least its womanly half. (RR p. 343)

VOLITION. From the standpoint of biology, every volition presupposes the existence of a binding force within the stream of the soul. (RR p. 478)

WORLD AND EXPERIENCE. That which we call the world, or, with more advanced reflection, the outer world, could never be experienced, still less could it be known, as that which it is without its alien character; and if Goethe is right when he declares

The eye could never see the sun,
If it had not a sun-like nature

then it is no less true that seeing and shining are as certainly and as fundamentally separate as it is that they must, in spite of this, be cognate. Accordingly, when we said that originally man rediscovers himself in the external world, this means precisely that he finds, by means of self-mirroring, the significance of the content of an intuited image, i.e., one that is alien to himself, and therefore immediately different from him, e.g., in the quantitative aspect. We immediately take the next step, however much it may seem to turn us from our goal. The saying that tradition has handed down to us from earliest times, that "astonishment is the beginning of all philosophy," announces with epigrammatic brevity the indispensable truth that it is precisely the unexpected (that which is dissimilar to the content of an explanation) which is pre-eminently fitted to stimulate reflection and, perhaps, to prepare it for discoveries; and the whole history of thought is there to demonstrate this truth. In a special sense, a fresh understanding of an alien character is invariably due to the fact that some animal or man did on some occasion behave in an essentially different manner from that which would have corresponded to our instinctive assumptions. (SW 4 pp. 209–10)

ON SCHOPENHAUER. "The World is my Representation!" But how do I go about employing a representation to create that which our philosopher, with such a parade of reasons, has utterly failed to demonstrate: the world?! (RR p. 360)

THE POLARITY OF LIFE. Life comprises the polarity of centripetal and centrifugal forces: this constitutes the true meaning of the terms *wandering* and *fixed*. Sometimes it entails conflict, as in the strife between the Amazonian element and the established-maternal one. Sometimes it is restricted to the ring forged by the sacred triad; at other times the pursuing elements embrace the incandescent horizon of the world. (RR p. 271)

MECHANISM AND METAPHYSICS. Mechanistic materialization can never be metaphysical. Whoever takes a balloon-flight into the atmosphere does not merge himself with the elements, as does the soul of the wanderer who communes with the clouds whilst his conscious body yet abides upon the soil of the earth. Herein lies the launching-point for the comprehension of a myriad mysteries: the *far*. (RR p. 305)

TYPES OF KNOWLEDGE. There is a knowledge that kills and a knowledge that awakens. The first can be seen in the verbal jugglery of our intellectuals; the second blossoms in the dithyrambic creativity of the poet and the visionary. As has been said of the latter type, he lives his life to the full as long as he inhabits the earth. He renews himself as if by a perpetual series of rebirths. The other sort is merely the mummified ash-heap of a once-living fire, the fossilized relic of a perished substance. His knowledge does produce mechanized results, but as he manipulates his carcasses, he speaks as if this dead matter were yet among the living. One sees with horror how he deludes himself into believing that he finds life only within his clockwork mechanisms. (RR p. 309)

HISTORICAL MODEL. Threefold model: the primordial-sleep-walking state in which decision and volition...have not yet be sundered; perhaps the best word for this stage would be *plant-like;* the second stage is the *magical,* during the course of which the priestly caste emerges. The third stage is the *mechanized,* which is dominated by deed, work, and science. (RR p. 311)

SANCTITY. Sanctity is always a symptom of physical pathology. The Christian saint: he has the look of a stage hypnotist, and his head is encircled by a faded ring! (RR p. 300)

CONCEPT AND LIFE. In every profound human countenance we see the traces of fear, horror, and sorrow. Modern man can reach no further with his concepts than he can with his experience. Everywhere life is without depth and dread, and all modern art is hollow. No man of depth can comprehend himself conceptually. Life is mystical. Life can never be frozen into rigid concepts. (RR p. 301)

WEEPING LIFE. Symbol of the highest rapture: the tear that bursts forth uncontrollably; the tear that "overflows" the eye. (RR p. 302)

THE WESTERN WORLD. Light and sound are the contrary poles of life. Sound binds the soul to the body, forming an essence that is proof against the opposition of the masses. Light is bodiless soul, eternal rest, and timeless being: *Nirvana.* — Light is Asia, sound is the West. Mediating between the two poles: color and ardor; they also mediate between Greece and Rome (RR p. 302)

PRIMORDIAL IMAGES AND MECHANIZATION. The primordial images *live;* this also means: they are powerful enough to ensure that no chance conceptual scheme will ever imprison them; it means also that they can incinerate, with the eyes of the sun, all those who would even attempt such a thing. On the other hand, nihilistic reason confuses the *signs* that accompany the inclusion of the primordial images with the *content* of this process; reason then beholds — instead of the image — a shape without substance. (RR p. 307)

ROME AND GERMANIA. In the substantial sense there is no "will to power." What has been falsely called by that name is actually the will to *expansion.* Rome's expansion was its will to power, and to a certain extent Rome's expansion manifested its egoism and self-interest. Rome's nature could not be approached, and it could never be conveyed beyond her borders because she demanded that everything had to be transported *into* Rome. The Roman will subjugated and wrecked all of her neighbors. The Germanic tribes arrived upon the scene too late, and that simple fact has decided the very destiny of the West. The Germans, the only people who had never known the meaning of the word "no," entered an already finished world. (RR p. 313)

THE LANGUAGE OF THE ORACLES. The future reveals itself only in images and symbols…But images and symbols communicate manifold meanings, and therefore they are often misunderstood. The history of the ancient world is replete with instances of falsely interpreted oracles. — The nature of the oracle is profoundly akin to that of poetry. (RR p. 317)

SAPPHIC WISDOM. Sappho prohibited all dirges and lamentations. This is how I interpret that fact: she prohibited the self-denial of the individual. The individual possesses the same abstract reality [*Realitaet*] as can be found in the conceptual *generality*. Only in the instant can there occur an unbounded actuality [*Wirklichkeit*]. (RR p. 317)

THE TIME OF THE DEAD. The time of the year when ghostly visitations occur is just before the onset of spring. The Greeks believed that the dead then strove to step once more into the light. (RR p. 318)

THE NATURE OF SPACE. The feeling for distance of the Romantics was the soul's awakening. Space is the visibility of the unified stream and its living resonance; the soul is itself the very tone of space. The Romantics' gazing into spatial distance constitutes a form of clairvoyance. In magical displays also, the *far* remains receptive to every *near*. (RR p. 320)

PRIESTS AND SCHOOLMASTERS. In Christianity, the priest conquered western mankind; in Socratism, this role was performed for us by the schoolmaster. That the Germans even now cannot relinquish Platonism is a consequence of the schoolmaster's spirit, in which Platonism has been planted so deeply. The priest gathers about him all the downcast natures. He attempts to elevate his flock by poisoning life itself. The schoolmaster gathers about him those who are vitally impoverished, upon whom he bestows an ersatz "rationality." In this way he empties life of its substance. (RR p. 346)

ON THE WISDOM OF LIFE. Commandments are always delivered first as prohibitions; *eventually* they receive an affirmative formulation. (RR p. 350)

ON CONNECTIONS I. The door to the room, towards which I gaze attentively, is *referred* to me, although I am not really connected with it; if, on the other hand, my wrist and the door knob were to be joined by a length of tape, I would then be connected with the door, regardless of whether I contemplated the door in question, or conjured up another within my imagination. The doorknob and the chair could be linked as well, although this connection would entail no relation. In order for me to conceive of the moon, I must first experience its light, and this is the case whether or not I am consciously aware of the fact. However, the moon is not influenced by the astronomer who scrutinizes her image. This applies to every *object* of perception in relation to the *process* of perception. (SW 2 p. 1143)

ON CONNECTIONS II. Whenever we find examples of connections that bind physical entities together, we always discover the mutuality of those connections. If I tug at the tape [that joins my wrist to the door knob], there occurs simultaneously the act of pulling at the tape and the effect that my action exerts upon the object with which the tape connects me. There is a marked difference between the aspect of an island as the sail boat approaches it, and its aspect as the sailor sets his foot on the island's shore. But in this case, only the bearer of perception can draw this distinction; the island cannot, of course, perceive the alteration of perspective, and the only evidence that any connection ever existed might be the sailor's footprints in the sands. (SW 2 p. 1143)

ON CONNECTIONS AND RELATIONS.

1. Connection is not relation.
2. Connections are inconceivable without reciprocal influences; relation does not entail influence.
3. Every connection is *real;* every relation is *mental.*
4. Connections are experienced directly, but cannot be comprehended; relations are comprehended, but cannot be directly experienced.

5. Connections are grounded in the actualities of the spatio-temporal continuum; relations are governed by *Spirit,* which is outside the spatio-temporal continuum.

6. Connections can occur without a cumulative series of relational steps; relations are never found without pre-requisite connections.

7. In order for a relation to occur, connections must be dissolved. (SW 2 p. 1144)

THE GENERAL AND THE PARTICULAR. The expressions "the tree existing absolutely" and "this particular tree in this particular place" are utterly unconnected, although there is a relationship between the general term and the particular. Thus, there is a relationship between the term and the object, but neither term nor object can be inferred from each other. The most penetrating critical sense runs aground when it attempts to derive the relationship of the *terms* from that of the *objects;* or, to reverse the direction of apprehension, to derive the relationship of the objects from that of the terms. The unavailing vehemence with which Plato attempted the latter procedure — and the attempts of his successors have fared no better than those of their master — has created difficulties for western philosophy throughout its history, for by utilizing thought's access to connections, Plato converted thinking into *appropriating.*

There are individual natures as well as elementary souls, which permit meaning to arise through the medium of their phenomenal appearance, without whose secret working power the very idea of connection would be restricted to the precincts of the "other world" of space. General terms can be applied to particular cases, since the meaning of the name, from which the concept is segregated, is, as it were, the promissory note of an essence, for which the boundary in question does not exist.

To the extent that the non-conceptual meaning concerns phenomenal characters, the area in which such entities operate already exists within them. It is only with the separation of the nature of the tree from the appearance of the tree, that the phenomenal tree can be distinguished from the noumenal; henceforth, conceptual relations usurp the place of real connections. The ground of their connection no longer lies within, nor can it be recovered once the entity has been stripped down to the status of a concept. That lost ground is: *actuality*. (SW 2 p. 1145)

RELATION AND PATTERN. The error that arises when we confuse real connections with merely conceptual relationships in representational forms, on which all remaining forms and cases equally depend, is the gradual, ceaseless disempowerment of the *name* that is promoted by the "logocentric" school of thought, during its 3,500 year quest to consummate the destruction of thought. Logocentric thought always pronounces its verdict in favor of the alleged reality of the concept or of the fact. In order to be able to preserve its faith in the reality of things, "naturalism" bases itself upon an unconscious (or conscious!) acceptance of the unification of name and concept through the agency of the thing.

In order to maintain its faith in the reality of concepts, "idealism" unconsciously (or consciously!) insists on the unification of name and thing through the agency of the concept ...

The following facts are easily comprehended: as mere *noumena*, concept and thing are related to each other, although they are not connected. The concept never relinquishes its nature, but the thing can so relinquish its nature, but only to the extent that it is visibly represented, since appearances that attain to the act of representation have the images at their disposal...There is a more spiritual act of apprehension, through which the fact and its concept arise together, i.e., in the act of will by which the name-meaning is severed from the name's conceptual sign. We may have an intuitive grasp of meaning, and we are free to choose any number of examples of such a grasp from the history of the sciences. Could we completely detach ourselves from the intuition of meaning (any attempt would certainly fail), then the name would have no more authentic connection than does a property label, a trade mark, a publisher's insignia, an "*ex libris*," or a badge of rank. This is, perhaps, an exaggeration, but it contains a measure of truth.

Assuming that the foregoing is true, we can easily show that both the "materialist" and "idealist" are willing to employ the idea of relations, in spite of the fact that they are unable rationally to account for their procedure. The scheme employed by the "idealist" at least deals with genuine contents of perception; but he cannot tell us just how it is that a perception arises. He is likewise unable to inform us as to just what links the perception and the name...(SW 2 pp. 1149–50)

THOUGHT AND SYMBOL. In symbolical thinking, the substantial entity and its type are identical. Along with the particular bird that has been chosen as a sacrificial victim, every bird belonging to its species is sacrificed, and the body of God that is eaten in the form of the communion wafer is one and the same, regardless of the fact that each believer partakes of a discrete wafer. (SW 2 pp. 1145–6)

SIMILARITY AND PERCEPTION. The world of perception is originally like a mirror that reflects man's image a thousand-fold, and therefore we must be on our guard all the more not to enter the blind alley of the so-called "projection" theory. In point of fact, that which we project into a phenomenon serves only to deceive, and only that which we correctly extract out of it serves the true interests of cognition. A lover returning from a happy encounter finds that all of the people whom he meets are more happy and more attractive than would ordinarily be the case: he has projected into them his own happiness and perfection, and has deceived himself just to this extent as to their real psychological disposition. Rightly considered, the phenomenon of "mirroring" shows us something utterly different. Essential cognition, or, more briefly, understanding, is possible only by virtue of some similarity between the perceiving self and the object of perception; as dissimilarity grows, understanding yields its place to a failure to understand, which at first is only felt, but later comes to be known (except in so far as by virtue of mere projection the gap is filled by *mis*understanding). Hence, we cannot be immediately certain whether the "savage" adores stones, trees, and animals; nor can we be sure that, instead of having projected something non-existent, he does not rather manifest a deeper understanding than our own. For it may be that his vitality is more vegetative in proportion as he has less personality than we; in that case, his judgments, or rather his attitudes, would have arisen on the basis of greater similarity or closer kinship, and this would have expressed something about the nature of stones, trees, and animals — albeit in mythical language — to which we later men have no access, because we have alienated ourselves from the mythopoeic realm. (SW 4 p. 208)

MEANING AND IMAGE. It seems that no one desires to comprehend the powers that are really at work in our world; nevertheless, one can name them, and, assisting in this naming (or, as would have been the case in earlier times, in the creating of symbols, a subject that must remain beyond our purview in this place) are those persons who have suffered the violent attentions of those powers to such a degree as to enable the victims to "summon to their memory" the events in question. What is revealed here, as the very idiom betrays, is the *name-meaning* (or the language-content). However, the mode of expression must be altered when we employ language to communicate the images that embody our most profound experiences. (SW 2 p. 1146)

THE MAGIC OF THE IMAGES. Magic has always been essentially a magic of images, and of all the forms of image-magic, the most popular is the one that has long been known throughout the world as the *charm,* from whose influence, even today, hardly anyone is completely free. (SW 2 p. 1146)

THE NAMES OF POWER I. For the ancient world, it was considered quite normal for even the most powerful of the gods to possess, in addition to their customary names, yet another name that had to be kept secret, for if anyone were to pronounce the secret name aloud, its very sound would annihilate the god. Ra, one of the highest gods in the Egyptian pantheon, announced to the world that he had summoned himself into existence merely by the act of pronouncing his secret name! Ra was eventually toppled from power when Isis tricked him into surrendering his secret name to the goddess. (SW 2 p. 1147)

THE NAMES OF POWER II.

The Islamic prophets who were in possession of the "great name" of their deity were powerful indeed. The name of Rome's guardian divinity was maintained in strictest secrecy so that no enemy, by hearing the name pronounced, would be able to press the god in question into the service of aliens who would thereby be enabled to seize control of Rome itself. (SW 2 p. 1147)

ON NAMING IN TRIBAL CULTURES.

The phenomenon [of the "names of power"] is encountered even today in a thousand shapes among the world's primitive and semi-primitive tribal cultures. Parents need not look far afield when selecting a name for their newly born baby, for the name is actually chosen, after investigation, by a member of the hereditary priesthood. In many cases, the name may not be pronounced, because this action might endanger the welfare of the child, who is therefore given a second name; even at the burial-site the names of totems are found far more frequently than the names of individuals (Tylor). In addition, should the name of the deceased be spoken aloud, the dead person would return as a spectral vampire. In that event, the name of the deceased, along with all similar-sounding names, would become taboo. Researchers have examined in great detail the significance of these facts as they affect the development, and the rapidity of transformation, of tribal languages. (SW 2 p. 1147)

WORD MAGIC.

Certain parties have pretended to locate the source of the phenomenon that we call "inspiration" in unseen forces, because the identical demand when pronounced by one mouth achieves results, and when pronounced by another mouth issues in failure. However, this phenomenon is certainly caused by accessory circumstances, such as the style of expression, the appearance and bearing of the speaker, and the "atmosphere" that colors the environment. In addition, there might be (not *must* be!) "fluids" exercising an influence in such cases. The Romantics considered such fluids to be manifestations of "life-magnetism." (SW 2 pp. 1147–8)

WORD AND SONG. When we witness the effect of the printed word, whether in diplomatic communication, in parliamentary negotiation, or in the oratory of the demagogue, we realize that there is very little direct influence at work in these instances. In primordial ages, the true power of the word resided in the performances of singers...Even during historical times, a condemned felon could often sing his way out of the prison cell and, on occasion, he might even receive high honors in recognition of his vocal talents! (SW 2 p. 1148)

LOVE IN THE WEST. Only those of Germanic blood can understand the true depths of love. The Oriental is too sensuous, the man of antiquity too self-controlled. The Greeks understood the inwardness of love better than did the Romans; nevertheless, the Greeks imprisoned Eros within forms. Love, not as passion, but as the harmony pervading the entire being of two persons; love, as the deep joy in another; and love, as warmth of heart and complete and devoted intimacy: that kind of love is Germanic. In Germanic man also there appeared for the first time true tenderness, the marvelous third element issuing from Spirit and desire. Here is devotion without dissolution of the self, mildness without weakness, pity without cruelty.

The Germanic nature, that perfect blend of every earthly element, was then ensnared and seduced by the Nazarenes' misuse of the word love... (RR p. 249)

WESTERN SUMMER, WESTERN WINTER. In summertime, the heavenly sky extends itself above our earth like a canopy. Palely gleaming stars are suspended from the shining dome, and the sickle moon dips low behind the horizon. No longer do the colors that radiate distance blossom in the western twilight. Warm and bright are the streaming rains that soon shroud the heavens. Now everything belongs to Gaia. It is the time when she feasts upon heat, electricity, and light. The ardent sun is sinking into her maternal waters…The Heraclitean fire sets out on his voyage from the universe to the earth.

In wintertime, the depths of nocturnal space are stirred. Through the violet-black wilderness of darkness roll the images of the stars. The cold, twinkling whiteness of the moon seems somehow drab; and, lost in the universe between the shifting constellations, Gaia plummets into the eternal night. The slanting sun sinks through a distance that seems as if it had been drained of its blood. At the North Pole, the Aurora Borealis blazes brightly. So we see that the earth is but a reeling ball thrown into the Uranian abyss. And as earth's fiery core thrusts outwards, the Heraclitean essence streams downwards. (RR p. 251)

PAGAN VOICES. Dark voices that speak out of the wind-tossed trees to the soul of the child, voices sounding like noisy children sharing a cart that jolts across the nocturnal heath. O dark voices: *no one fears you now.* (RR p. 255)

MAN AND EARTH. From the outset I choose the people that will be important to me based on my ability to view them as if they were fragments of the earth, as if they will be to me as soil, forest, cloud, rock, noble blood, smoldering summer, or spring breeze. Other sorts must remain outside the telluric round-dance, for they are *anthropocentric*, and, therefore, they themselves constitute the sickness that infects the earth. The Moloch's belly in which these spiritually diseased characters house themselves is — *the big city.* (RR p. 256)

EROS OF THE DISTANCE. The essence of all true love is: the Eros of the distance ([Alfred] Schuler). Love is the most profound strangeness, the utterly vexing riddle, the flaming vision approaching from unknown horizons, the eternal mystery. Love perishes when one removes the veil that conceals its secret. Yearning, which dreams of possession, is the essence of love. Nothing earthly can compare with our first thrilling encounter with the beloved...(RR p. 258)

FROM A DIARY ENTRY. How do these people manage to thrust themselves between me and the universe?! (RR p. 265)

FROM EROS TO PLATO. With the advent of Eros at the second creation of the world, there also appeared a fresh danger for life. Erotic life is psychical, and psychical life is richer in woe and closer to death than is the life that yet remains within an incoherent chaos...The breakdown [of erotic life] took place in Greece. The same stream leads directly from Thracian Dionysus to Orphic Lesbos; but between Lesbos and Plato a great abyss has opened up. That which was formerly viewed as the release of demonic powers from the chains forged by *things,* has, in Plato, become the liberation of the transcendental ego from the bonds of the *body.* (RR p. 268)

LIFE IN THE INDIVIDUAL; LIFE IN THE STRANGER. The may be a peculiar strength in one who experiences only himself. His inner radiance may at times even cast the light outside him into deep shadow. Nevertheless, we often find that this is accompanied by limitation, weakness, and an excessive ardor that may eventually separate him from the totality and render him incapable of movement. How the universe is experienced by the individual means: how he participates in its *eternal flux.* This is the reason why we find authentic symbols of life in such kindred phenomena as high spirits, warmth, heat, love, respect, and devotion... Such phenomena arouse a pulsating current between ego and world. In willing and yearning, on the other hand, there is merely *tension.* (RR p. 316)

THE DUALITY OF FEELINGS. Every feeling bears its polar opposite within itself. The man who strives to amass power obviously wishes to enjoy the feeling of domination; but in order fully to understand the feeling of domination, he must at the same time understand the feeling of *subjugation* to another's power. In every feeling, there is a striving from something *here* to something *there*. The first point and the last point determine the *direction* of the striving. (RR p. 331)

THE POISON. From the outset, Christianity poured the poison of transcendence into the waters of the pagan underworld. (RR p. 290)

THE SEVEN BASIC DISPOSITIONS OF INDIVIDUAL LIFE.
First, the still undivided substance; second, the substance bifurcates into the life of matter and the life of Spirit; third, the substance with a ruling direction towards Spirit; fourth, the substance with a ruling direction towards matter; fifth, an insubstantiality joining matter and Spirit; sixth, insubstantial matter; and, seventh, insubstantial Spirit. (RR p. 481)

ON THE DOCTRINE OF LIFE. The metaphysics of life rests upon three pillars: life is eternal distance (symbolized by the wheel); life is the *panta rhei* (symbolized by the flood; and life is image (symbolized by the mirror). (RR p. 295)

ON MELCHIOR PALAGYI. We would be hard-pressed to improve upon Palagyi's monumental proposition: "The one source from which springs every possible human error is to be found in our seeing the spiritual in what is actually living, and in seeing living substance in what is merely spiritual." Scornful of both "rationalism" and "sensualism," from the outset he centered his research upon the separation and distinction of Spirit from life. He, and nobody else, re-discovered the natural-scientific *theory of life* (also called "neo-vitalism"), which he first elaborated as a counter-position to every possible theory of Spirit. He banished the drab twilight of so-called "epistemology" with the penetrating clarity of his research into the underlying grounds that render consciousness possible. (SW 3 p. 741)

THE LEGACY OF PAGANISM. The pagan urn is shattered; war has raged around the shards, and the fragments have been scattered to the winds. Now the vampire of mankind, the Jew, appears on the scene. He knows not the meaning of this urn, and he certainly cannot restore it to its original condition. But he is aware, of course, that it represents a price-less treasure. So he makes off with the melancholy and lovely fragments, which he then arrays in a gaudy, vulgar setting. It will end up adorning some Jewess. (RR p. 281)

TYPES OF ANGER. The anger of the Asian is black, that of the German is blue; the first appears uncanny, the second profound. Asiatic anger occurs sporadically, either in silence or accompanied by the most inhuman screams; he stabs, he impales, he crucifies, he gluts himself with cruelty and torture, before he kills. The angry German is like a tempest of crushing blows, he is convulsed by a roaring frenzy, and he will run out of steam only when everything within reach has been smashed to pieces — recall Thor and his hammer! (RR p. 286)

THOUGHT AND SPIRIT. Spirit is silent. Whenever a concept appears it is cloaked in the spoken word — there are no unspoken or non-symbolic concepts. The concept is akin to Spirit in that both are alien to the world of images. Only when Spirit is cast out of the body can radiance emerge into the visible realm; only in the mediated element will Spirit become thought and, finally, concept. (RR p. 286)

ESSENCE. The essence is the garb of the cosmic fire; the process comprises its inner assimilation and elimination through the individual nature; and its road leads from the universe into the ego. The inner ac-cumulation of the essence occurs through the sensuous satisfaction of in-tense passion. The cell performs the essential work of assimilation, and its symbols are the hearth, the site of the nurturing fire; the house, the family vault, the crypt, the catacombs: in brief, everything maternal. The cell is cosmic in so far as it divides its substance, and allows its life to stream outwards. (RR p. 250)

SYMBOLS. False doctrines are the culprits that first instilled the poison of mistrust and unbelief into the gentle, weary souls of the Hellenes, and ever since that time the gallows and the torture-rack have stood as the threatening symbols before the gates of life. (RR p. 243)

COSMIC FLAME. There is a profound difference between the yellow flame and the livid blue one, as there is between the naphtha-flame and the lightning, or between the will-o'-the-wisp and St. Elmo's fire. This is the opposition between essence and void, between the body pulsing with blood and the astral body, between earthly and celestial fire, between phlogiston and ether, between the hot flame and the cold. Out of the union of aether and gravity arose the essence-as-body. Christianity was the process of separating aether from gravity, light from heat, celestial body from telluric body. Christianity turned the ancient gods into sorcerers and ghosts. (RR p. 244)

THE RUSH OF INTOXICATION. Only during highly cultured epochs can Eros be experienced as the *rush*. Certainly, the constant intoxication that characterize "primitive" cultures differs profoundly from the second degree of intoxication, which is felt to be an overwhelming, turbulent, and shattering invasion of consciousness. (RR p. 245)

THE GERMAN TRAGEDY. Germany did not take her soul from the integral Cosmos, but she did take her disposition from a half-strangled one: the fractured lines of its medieval style, the fruitless struggle of her thinkers with the object, and the gigantism of her modern cities. On the other hand, one can discover the darkly groping, pulsating side of her cosmic soul in Germany's villages, in her isolated farmsteads, and — most of all — upon her moorlands. (RR p. 254)

EPIC ARTISTRY. The genuine artist does not traffic in fictions. The demonic powers that he sings, speaks, or forms, are *there*. In plastic embodiment the wave is image *and* event. — The cosmic epic poet reunites that which has been sundered: the epic world-poem to the "ardor of the eye." He steps out of the modern age and spins the golden threads of the eternal flux. A god and a lightning-bolt will not suffice — the entire history of the gods must unfold before his gaze. (RR p. 254)

THE POET AND THE MAN OF ACTION. We are not men of action; we are not obligated to lay siege to forbidden realms. We live in accord with the necessities of nature, we struggle in accord with the necessities of the day. Our blood may beat against the stars, but it spills itself fruitlessly in the dust of the gutter.

The man of action pays no heed to chatter about obstacles in his path; he sees only ever-new objectives that he must conquer. He is aroused by opposition, since he anticipates the intoxication of conquering his foes.

The dreamer and the man of action will always be *opposites*. (RR p. 254)

ON THE ARTIST. Work is act and act is Spirit. Art is an activity and, hence, derives from Spirit. The artist may become an eccentric individualist with a gigantic ego, but he remains bound to the heart of the earth. We employ two criteria in estimating his artistic power: the quantum of artistic fire that he has summoned from the earth, and the extent to which he has distanced himself from mediocrity. (RR p. 257)

THROUGH LIFE. After endless searching, one trembles to discover: the painted exterior of things, their meaning and nature. Through a transparent veil one sees a second world that becomes a metaphysical reality. Causes and effects constitute a puppet-show for the blindness of our thought. Behind it all, however, there is the living universe, stirred by the beating wings of the gods: I experience it in the storms of youth, I lose it during the age of temptation, I comprehend it in the autumn of my thought. (RR p. 255)

THE NATURE OF THE POET. Although the poet remains an individual, he remains still an aspect of the cosmic flux: he is animal, star, sea, plant; he is the eye of the elements; he is matriarchal and earthly to the core. The praxis by which he expresses his inner vision is *magic* (RR p. 261)

JEAN PAUL [RICHTER]. Jean Paul is a texture, not a structure. (RR p. 307)

ON DUALITIES. One duality is that of subject and object. The growing emancipation of the object is intertwined with the weakening of the instincts. — The duality of body and soul is a completely different matter, however. The origin of this duality lies in sexuality, and it intensifies with the division between the sexes, until, finally, our species is split into two halves. The first symptom of consciousness: that man differentiates between himself and his sexual organs and, thus, between his higher and his lower drives. (RR p. 303)

FALSE SYMBOLS. What could be an emptier production than the Symbolists' anthropocentric interpretation of the cosmos, or their compulsion to dress up ugly bodies in the vacant remnants of life! The whole Symbolist racket is a usurpation of the throne by the spawn of bankers. It began with excessive ornamentation, and with such excesses it will end. First: you build your house. Second: you hang up your tapestries. Then Stefan George moves in. (RR p. 304)

MECHANISTIC AND MAGICAL PHILOSOPHY. Magic is the praxis of our philosophy, and our philosophy is the theory of magic. The philosophy that is taught by the professors is invariably mechanistic, and the attendant praxis is always mechanical. — Magical philosophy repudiates the thesis of identity; consequently, it repudiates unity, thing, duration, repetition, and mathematics. My philosophy also repudiates concept and causation, for causation is the theoretical parallel to the logical nexus. — Magical philosophy works with images and symbols, and its method is that of analogy. — The most important names here are: element, substance, principle, demon, cosmos, microcosm, macrocosm, essence, image, primal-image, whirlpool, the orb, and the fire. — Its ultimate formulas are incantations that have all of the power of magic at their disposal. (RR p. 312)

LOVE AND THE FAR. We love what is strange, but only to the extent that we glimpse within it the person that we once were in the most rapturous moments of youth, or in a superhuman, or even a godlike, previous life. *All love is Eros of the distance.* (RR p. 289)

DOWNFALL. The ancient world shattered the primordial order of things when it imprisoned the demonic matriarchal powers in the chthonic depths and elevated the daylight masculine world of Spirit to supreme power. (RR p. 290)

ON BACHOFEN AS "THE GREATEST LITERARY EXPERI-ENCE." In Bachofen we have to recognize perhaps the greatest interpreter of that primordial mentality, in comparison with the cultic and mythic manifestations of which, all later religious beliefs and doctrines appear as mere reductions and distortions. ("Appreciation" [*Wuerdigung*] in J. J. Bachofen, *Versuch ueber die Graebersymbolik der Alten,* ed. C. A. Bernoulli [Basel: Helbing & Lichterhahn, 1925], pp. x-xi.)

ON THE "MORTUARY SYMBOLISM" OF J. J. BACHOFEN. I rank this book among the supreme spiritual achievements in the history of mankind. For more than twenty-five years, I have found in Bachofen the man who has guided the course of my life. (LK GL p. 225)

BACHOFEN'S GREATEST ACHIEVEMENT. It was J. J. Bachofen who, in his two masterworks *Mother Right* and *Mortuary Symbolism* (along

with the scarcely less important *The Lycians* and *The Myth of Tanaquil*),
was able for the first time successfully to interpret the entire prehistory
of the West from the standpoint of the battle between "matriarchy" and
"patriarchy." (SW 3 p. 494)

BACHOFEN'S DUALITY. The matriarchal and the hetairic prin-
ciples. The first is fixed: tribal, established, and traditional. The second is
wandering, solitary, hostile to all settled modes of association. The first, by
necessity, experiences the eternal and encompassing destiny that governs
all happenings. — The second lives with doom and the annihilation of all
at the hands of death. The disentangling of these antitheses can reveal a
higher unity than may be apparent amid all the struggle and destruction.
So, the settled-matriarchal principle struggles against the wandering-
hetairic principle. The transformation into morality occurs steadily; it
happens more effortlessly for the fixed principle than for the wandering
one. (RR p. 312)

THE WORK. Whatever within us becomes embodied in our work,
no longer belongs to us. The insight, the work of art, and the deed must
henceforth live only for themselves. (RR p. 300)

TIME AND THE PRIMORDIAL. As against the customary notion
of time, primordial time incarnates the primal flux. Whatever has been
immersed within this flux will shine with the aura of the elemental and
the eternal. Death first came to those born in the primordial world not as
the result of a great flood that somehow severed modern man's ties with
the primal order: that task was performed by the invasion of the world by
the void known as "transcendence."

That "transcendence" severs subject from object and body from soul,
just as it rends the body of time. One half of time foists upon us that
false "eternity," which, in truth, is an "always" that is forever outside the
temporal dimension; whilst the other half is divorced from the spatial di-

mension. In this way, space is stripped of its soul, and time is stripped of its body. (RR p. 351)

"MONISM." All of historical mankind has been raised in the philosophy of "monism." The belief in the laws of causality, and in legality generally, is monistic. All thinking activity is monistic…The monistic philosophy easily explains the origins of all of the world's religions, the distinctive qualities of human societies, the causal laws that govern our dream-life, etc. *And every one of us is infected by this madness!* (RR p. 351)

ON HYSTERIA. The hysterical person lives within his dreams, day and night, and he is powerless and lifeless throughout his waking hours. One peculiar manifestation: his sexual life, because it is devoid of Eros, is compelled to produce disturbances in his conscious mind as well as in his body…His life, as it were, belongs to dreams that have no basis in perception, and, thus, his life belongs to phantoms. He can only be released in one of two ways: through the destruction of his dream world, or through his entry into the real world. The task of the therapist should be to *realize* the Eros of the hysterical character. (RR p. 357)

ON THE ACHIEVEMENT OF C. G. CARUS. Today we live in an age of joyless haste, an age that more or less shatters everything in its savage maelstrom. Faint of heart, and scarcely comprehending what we see, we stand before such an abundantly fruitful life as that of Carus, a life that required no monastic seclusion, a life that resembled a gigantic tree that shoots out branches on all sides without degenerating. We may remind ourselves at this time of similar monuments of the past, and we understand clearly that the gains accruing to our power-crazed rulers must infallibly entail heavy losses in the soul and in creativity! (AC p. 310)

THE PELASGIAN STATE OF MIND. Just as no one can determine precisely how much of the story of the Trojan War as it is told to us in the *Iliad*, along with its prologue and sequel, is founded upon strict factuality, so no one can determine precisely how much of that which we are told by the ancient writers about the "Pelasgian World" is founded upon strict factuality. However, even were historical criticism to demonstrate conclusively that the Pelasgians existed only in legendary lore, one thing would still be established beyond the shadow of a doubt: that the "Pelasgian" state of mind, among other things also found in the myths, belongs to the irreducible facts of prehistory. Just as according to our doctrine of the "actuality of the images" every individual, as well as every cultural period, participates in the world-image through the image-shaping powers of the soul, we must, therefore, establish every manifestation of man's inner life within the realm of facts in order to understand the world-image and, with it, the religious beliefs of those whom we are studying...Indeed, without a knowledge of such inner realities and their formal operations, we cannot understand even the brute facts of ages to which scholarship has applied the prejudicial epithet "historical." (SW 2 p. 1251)

WAR AND THE STATE. Man has existed in an uninterrupted state of war ever since the first state was founded, and the horror of warfare has grown along with the growth of the powers of the state, regardless of whether a particular war is waged between states, races, classes, vocations, sects, or discrete groups within the state. Obviously, the *bellum omnium contra omnes* ("the war of all against all") is not something that characterizes the state of nature, for it is only since man has taken up residence within the state that he has waged that endless series of wars that constitutes "world history." Hegel was quite correct when he said that the Spirit could only realize its potential within the state; but Nietzsche was also correct, from a different perspective, in saying that he found in Spirit the "will to power," and in saying that the state was the "coldest of all cold monsters." (AG p. 177)

THE MACHINE. The English "Deists," led by Sir Isaac Newton, that master of the mechanistic apocalypse, openly proclaimed that the world must have had a divine origin, since it so obviously possesses the character of a purposeful machine (recall that Kant was still impressed by the so-called physico-theological proof of the existence of God!).

We know of no better way to illustrate the appalling unnaturalness of our apostles of political and moralistic "progress," who are so intoxicated by the pseudo-life of the machine, than to adduce two words of wisdom which were attributed to Zhang Zhou, and which encapsulate more than two millennia of Chinese philosophical culture: A conceited traveler sees a gardener in a trench drawing buckets of water with which he is irrigating his plot of vegetables; the traveler advises the gardener to invest in a machine that will do his work for him. The gardener laughs and says: "This I have heard from my teacher: the cunning have tools and show their cunning in business, and those who are cunning in business have cunning in their hearts, and those who have cunning in their hearts cannot remain pure and uncorrupted, and those who do not remain pure and uncorrupted are restless in Spirit, and those who are restless in Spirit are those in whom the Tao can find no dwelling-place. It's not that I do not understand the tools of which you speak. *It's just that I would be ashamed to use them.*" The other anecdote goes as follows: The Spirit of the clouds asks the whirlpool why everything upon the earth has ended up in such a disordered state. The whirlpool answers: "That the order of the world is shattered, that the conditions of life are thrown into confusion, that the will of heaven is without effect, that the animals of the field are driven away, that birds screech in the night, that mildew rots the trees and the plants, that destruction overwhelms everything that crawls upon the earth: all that is the fault of *government*." (AG pp. 181–2)

THE "TUIST" (OPPOSITE POLE TO THE "EGOIST"). The relationship of the "tuist"[2] to his fellow man makes up the most essential part of his life. From the outset he makes his position clear to his associ-

---

2   Tuist is a term coined by Klages. The distinction between tuist and egoist entails a recognition of the characterological distinction between those whose drives and affects are focused on the "you," as opposed to those who are centered solely upon their own ego.

ates and he lives in a conscious sense only for others. What he means to them is decisive for him: he will be loved or he will rule. Passionate desire alternates with tyrannical will. His personal feelings are revealed in all of his actions, and so he will show the greatest interest only in those sorts of activities that provide him with the opportunity to take a personal part in the arrangements. He inclines to artistic and quasi-artistic vocations; should he devote himself to science, his decision would result from deep needs arising out of his personal ambition. In addition, he will occasionally devote his efforts to political life, the public welfare, and economic conditions; then we get the propagandist, the world-improver, and the prophet. He is not in the least indifferent to outward appearances, and when he gets the opportunity he will indulge in theatrical behavior. In many ways, his bearing resembles that of a woman. The typical woman is always a "tuist." (SW 4 p. 4)

ON THE PROGRESS-PHILISTINE. Listen to him chattering about how far "we" have come, how wonderful is the time in which "we" live, and how delightful are the gadgets that are available to "us"…Everything that he says sounds like the babbling of a carnival conjuror; everything that he says reveals the utter impotence of his Spirit! (SW 2 p. 1543)

APOLLO'S CULT. The cult of Apollo is the cult of the beautiful. This phenomenon occurred only once, if we are not mistaken, i.e., in *Greece*; it lasted for a mere three centuries; and no other people and no other time has managed to achieve anything like it — not even the "Renaissance" — although the *yearning* for the Greek ideal of beauty has persisted down to our own time. (AC p. 382)

WILHELM JORDAN AND SCHOPENHAUER. From our earliest days we have delighted in the poet Jordan's essay "Encounters with Schopenhauer," which was published in the collection entitled *Letters and Lectures*. All those who admire Schopenhauer (and all Schopenhauer scholars as well) will profit from the reading of this dazzling memoir, which, along with many verbatim transcriptions of Schopenhauer's speech, provides us with the most perceptive portrayal of the person and the life of the thinker. The author also recounts discussions that took place when Schopenhauer and Jordan were joined by Friedrich Hebbel! (AC p. 385)

THE MANIFOLD VOICES OF GOETHE. Occasionally we hear of certain similarities between Nietzsche and Schiller. We admit that it is always possible to establish connections between the works of important authors. Thus, it is true that both Schiller and Nietzsche consistently employed dramatic rhetoric (although the differences between the characteristic rhetoric of the two men are enormous); it is also true that everything that the two men wrote reveals a consummate mastery of *style.* Now we ordinarily think of a stylist as one whose language possesses an unprecedented force and unity. But there is another approach to this matter of style: *Goethe's.* Goethe's narrative prose in *Werther* — which is well-nigh incomparable — deviates perceptibly from the narrative prose of the *Elective Affinities;* and his deftly controlled speech in the "*Fuellest wieder Busch und Tal*" and Mignon's *Lied* deviates sharply from that of the *Diwan* or the second part of *Faust.* (AC p. 388)

MORALITY. Moralistic activity, properly speaking, is *reactivity.* Only instinct that attains to consciousness is truly productive. — Likewise, the nothingness [*das Nichts*] that is the ego possesses the drive to permanence and the "will to power." The function of that will is to convert everything into *thought.* (RR p. 300)

CONSCIOUSNESS AND LIFE. The ultimate depth is naïve; it is the immediate, instinctual *now.* Whatever is completely alive cannot comprehend its true nature. Every increase of consciousness entails an abandonment of life. (RR p. 300)

DIONYSIAN RADIANCE. Dionysian man *lives* his dream-images. Rays of light stream forth from his soul into the world, and whoever wanders into his radiant sphere shines with his love. (RR p. 300)

"MATTER AND FORM." Spirit disintegrates substance into "Matter and Form." Birth alone is the primordial; birth alone is the cosmic substance [*Hyla*] itself, the primeval mother. The sculptor, however, seeks to ensnare the two halves of the duality [*dyas*], to re-unite matter and form. He is seized by an instinctual compulsion, and his Spirit strives to revert to the primordial womb out of which substance emerged. But his aspiration is a fatal option, doomed to a perpetual *perishing*. (RR p. 309)

THE GERMANIC INSTINCT. The instinct of other peoples is weak or non-existent; the German has instinct, but it is *blind*. On this account, he becomes the man of science, the man of firm convictions, the man of principles, the man who derives his steadfast faith in morality from books. He *must* remedy his lack of knowledge through study; he is compelled to surmount his insecurity of will through partisanship. (RR p. 339)

SCIENCE AND METAPHYSICS. There has never been, nor will there ever be, a truly great scientist who is utterly devoid of metaphysics. And the scientist is never more deeply under the sway of his metaphysical presuppositions than when he is unaware of their very existence. (SW 6 p. 539)

FAITH AND DOUBT. Knowledge does not arise from faith, but from doubt, i.e., the very *negation* of faith. (RR p. 352)

"IDEALISM" AND "REALISM." For those students who find the technical philosophical terms in current use to be somewhat alien, but who are somewhat better acquainted with the various warring "isms" of the day, we will, for obvious psychological purposes, simplify somewhat the various points of view at issue by arranging the diverse schools of thought under the two headings of "idealism" and "realism." On the side of "idealism" we have: rationalism, criticism, subjectivism, "logical positivism," "fictionalism," "solipsism," etc.; on the side of "realism" we place: "sensualism," "empiricism," "atomism," "materialism," etc. The representatives of "idealism" always claim that they understand the inner life — and even life itself! — from the standpoint of Spirit; the representatives of "realism" are equally certain that they understand these things by examining impressions and experiences and, ultimately, being. But since Spirit and being are intimately connected as subject and object, the opposition between the two groups of "isms" is utterly irrelevant (except, that is, for those who insist on rehashing empty controversies regarding the existence — or non-existence — of "innate ideas"). (AC p. 384)

THE SENTIMENTAL EGOIST. There is one type of egoism that we will call "the egoism of the sentimental." The egoism of the sentimental person manifests itself most blatantly in an overwhelming desire to be loved. Such persons are usually contented with their worldly wealth and status; but when it comes to affairs of the heart they will reveal an extreme pretentiousness. Quite often they will be driven by a dangerous compulsion to rely excessively on others, a condition that can develop into species of psychical vampirism that can suck the life out of those to whom they have attached themselves. The *reactive* manifestation of this egoism is a capacity for intense jealousy. (AC p. 377)

THE DIONYSIAN. The body is the day-pole of the inner life, or the center of vision and appearance. When perception governs, the dream-image must, perforce, fade away. Not only the Spirit, but the body as well, stands in opposition to the untrammeled growth of the soul. For that reason, the authentic expression of Dionysian ecstasy is the rending of the god's body. (RR p. 288)

ROMANTICISM AND POLARITY. The Romantics distinguished between the day-pole and the night-pole of the soul. This distinction pointed to the polar relationship between the dreaming and the waking states of consciousness. In the night-pole, instinct, yearning, clairvoyance, telepathy, sooth-saying, dream, poetry, art, and magic have their roots; in the day-pole, we locate thinking and willing. The night-pole bespeaks woman, left, night, moon, and ganglion; the day-pole bespeaks man, law, day, and the brain. But what the Romantics were unable to clarify is the central capacity of the night-pole: the gift of vision, out of which, as from an ocean, emerges a primal flux, an unending stream of influences and impressions...(RR p. 288)

DAY AND NIGHT. In day-consciousness we perceive, but in night-consciousness we experience visions. Only into day-consciousness could the a-cosmic Spirit erupt. (RR p. 289)

ROCOCO AS "VIRTUAL REALITY" (VIRTUELLE REALITAET) [WRITTEN IN 1913]. Rococo has the virtual reality of a mirror image, the mere appearance; every sound, scent, and shimmering light of its landscape is the reflection of a mask. (RR p. 292)

SO-CALLED "SYNTHETIC THOUGHT." Every so-called synthesis of thought arises from the impulse to revive distinctions that analysis has already enforced, and thus, this impulse is only one more expression of the monistic compulsion to force the vital manifold into the unity demanded by Spirit. (RR 364)

THE WISDOM OF THE ROMANTICS. Although the Romantics were not completely free of logocentric errors, the bright atmosphere of their soul-born wisdom shone more deeply into the nocturnal depths of the cosmos than the efforts of all previous mystics; it is, above all, the Heraclitean concept of polarity which enabled these vibrant spirits to clarify not merely the millennial traditions of myths and symbols: the Romantics also sought to undermine the threat of an arrogant material-ism by their employment of the alkahest ["universal solvent"]of the soul. When, therefore, the Romantics utilized the magnetic electric pole as an illustrative example in their speculations, we must not forget that the discovery of this type of polarity, which was credited to Volta, although it actually belongs to Ritter, was, in fact, a Romantic achievement. (SW 2 p. 890)

GERMANIC ROMANTICISM. Romanticism flourished in the Germanic world, and only in that world. Romanticism reached its highest peaks, and sent its roots most deeply into the earth, in Germany... We must always bear in mind that the greatest achievement of the Romantics was to embrace every field of the Spirit, and especially the philosophy of nature, within its charmed circle. There was a Romantic astronomy, physics, chemistry, mineralogy, geology, paleontology, botany, zoology, osteology, physiology, medicine, pharmacology, and even, to a certain extent, a Romantic mathematics. Now what has any of that to do with "foreign" influences? (SW 2 pp. 888–9)

GOETHE AND THE ROMANTICS. Literary Romanticism began with the *Sturm und Drang* of the late eighteenth century. Romantic entries — along with other material of the most superficial quality — can be found in Heinse, Herder, and Hamann, as well as in all of the vitalistic nature-philosophy of the period. On the other hand, there appears even in Goethe's universalism a component that is recognizably Romantic, and of which he was most certainly aware, for this component had a profound impact on more than one Romantic philosopher of nature; it would one day function as the guiding principle of C. G. Carus's world-view. Goethe was always impressed by the concept of the primal phenomenon, a concept that enabled Goethe to direct his scientific attention not to primal things, but to primal *images*. In opposition to the mechanistic philosophy of nature, and to rigid explanatory schemes in general, it was the living content of the perceived entity that preoccupied Goethe; his worldly sensuality enabled him to focus upon the visually grasped images, to which his words of truth always referred. No doubt, he was interested in every aspect of nature, but his studies always led him back to that which he had "perceived through the senses." His studies of nature, he says elsewhere, rested "on a purely experiential basis"; and in the *Proverbs in Prose* occurs the following brilliant proposition which, at one stroke, shatters the idealistic errors of the millennia: "People seek only nothingness behind phenomena: for the phenomena themselves are the theory!" (SW 2 p. 889)

THE ARROGANCE OF RATIONALISM. The modern disciple of the faith in the omnipotence of reason can hardly restrain his joy as he babbles into our ears his conviction that he now possesses a *logic* of the "unconscious!" (SW 1 p. 231)

LITERATURE AND THE PATHIC SOUL. *Peer Gynt,* Ibsen's great creation, although not purely poetic, certainly unfolds the shifting panorama of a thoroughly pathic approach to life. The characters whose psychical abysses are illumined by Dostoyevsky are, without exception, pathics, who go marching straight to doom. Here we have everything that the student of sick souls could possibly desire: from the "flight" into the night of forgetfulness, through the "twilight condition," to the "split personality," unconscious behavioral tactics, somnambulism, and seeming acts of unsurpassed purposefulness, without — or even against — the will of the actor.

One example: Raskolnikov [in *Crime and Punishment*], shortly after his murderous rampage, staggers around his city, utterly without purpose — or so he thinks — driven by hostility to all human associations. "Every encounter aroused his loathing, the faces of people were as abhorrent as their gestures and their movements...When he arrived at the quay of the Neva on Vasilievsky island, he stood upon the bridge. 'Here's where he lives, in this very house,' thought Raskolnikov, 'but I have not come here of my own accord to Rasumichin!'"...Who can read this chapter through without being struck by its precise rendering of "post-hypnotic suggestion?" (SW 1 p. 233)

ON THE HERACLITEAN FLUX. Just as the Eleatics had discovered being, it was Heraclitus who discovered actuality, which he renders in the world-renowned formula: "All things are in flux" [*panta rhei*]; the flux is the very essence of the world, or, in other words, the world is a happening without a substrate. Heraclitus is not, however, content merely to theorize about the eternal stream, for he also discovers in the world-process the phenomenon of rhythm; in other words, he is the discoverer of polarity. With the aid of that concept, he clarifies the semblance of existence [*Dasein*] of that which endures as analogous to what we today would call "stationary equilibrium," i.e., the equilibrium of two contra-directed processes.

For Heraclitus, everything is alive. To him both the living and the dead truly live. Both the living and the dead are but formal manifestations of the primordial life of the world itself. And here we encounter a discovery which distinguishes the speculations of this outstanding philosopher from those of all previous thinkers: the idea that individual life, as the form of arrested, or deficient, life — which takes the "road upwards" to attain to dissolution — can, on the other hand, lead to the highest liberation and to the greatest vital plenitude as well. Thus, death appears as a liberation to a loftier form of cosmic life, as opposed to a temporally-restricted organic existence [*Dasein*]. Furthermore, sleep as the mediating transition to death, can be seen as a prototype of a fulfilled vitality…Hitherto, the doctrine of Heraclitus has been seen as emerging "all of a piece," and this doctrine is, admittedly, the most profound of all philosophical systems. Sadly, however, even this philosopher of cosmic life went off the rails when he dragged in the theory of the *logos*…which he calls an ordering, rationalizing, regulating power, a "law" decreed by the transcendent ruler "Zeus." And this is not just the misuse of a word! (SW 6 pp. XVII–XVIII)

CHARACTER AND IDEALS. The common viewpoint that holds that we can derive a person's ideals from his character, stands opposed to the conviction that a person prefers and seeks precisely that which he does not possess; without a doubt, the second viewpoint holds the greater measure of truth. The gentlest woman desires a man who is courageous, strong, and heroic (and vice versa); the poet who delights in the narration of orgies worthy of Messalina, is often found to be living on bread and water in an attic chamber; and a scholar of genius like Mommsen, who scrutinizes the deeds of great statesmen with the most rigorous and critical acumen, is himself the most superficial and mediocre politician on the planet. (SW 6 p. 28)

PIOUS IDEALS. With "good intentions," pious wishes," and enduring illusions, we arrive at those abstractions that determine the limits of the outer, as well as the inner life. Ideals are undoubtedly elements of character, but they are elements torn from natural connections of every sort, and for that reason they are divorced from the facts...Man's ideals clearly reveal how rich he is: *in poverty.* (SW 6 pp. 28–9)

SPIRIT AND ITS MANIFESTATIONS. The Spirit, as it functions in modern scientific research, is only one division — or, more correctly, one phenomenal manifestation — of the identical Spirit that has ripened into the modern state and modern capitalism. (SW 1 p. 128)

NIHILISM. "Panlogism," Kantianism, and Sensualism: they are but three varieties of one and the same nihilism, three modes, or methods, whereby an invading force from outside the cosmos annihilates the cosmos of images. (SW 1 p. 173)

THE "LAST OF THE MOHICANS." The hour of reaction has been missed; there are those among us whose passionate love of life has made them see just how wretched the world has become: we are the "last of the Mohicans." Whoever still has it in him to express a wish, must wish for one thing above all: that the consummately vile mankind of today may drown, die, disappear as soon as possible, along with his wretched arsenal of murder, so that once again the forests may resound with the roar of purifying and self-renewing winds. (SW 1 p. 768)

PHILOSOPHICAL CONFUSION. The Eleatics were guilty of confusing actuality with being; however, the logician manifests an even greater confusion when he mistakes actuality for truth. The logician is led by his Parmenidean impulse to the most arrogant of all errors when he equates actuality itself with the mere *thought* of actuality. There are no independent "propositions-in-themselves," such as Bolzano desired, just as there are no "truths-in-themselves," such as his modern acolytes craved. Within the thinking consciousness of the individual there are neither truths nor propositions, but only fleeting manifestations of inconceivable happenings. (SW 1 p. 86)

"Psychology" and "Epistemology" ["Theory of Cognition"].

Basically, everything that our professors insist on calling "psychology" is an unavowed "epistemology," just as the so-called "epistemology" of the professors could, with equal justice, call itself "psychology." The whole matter shall not have been devoid of a certain humorous flavor should the discussion ultimately come to focus upon the question as to where, in fact, the precise boundary between the two disciplines is to be drawn. (SW 1 p. 218)

The Limits of Education.

The individual's capacity to acquire education is governed by natural limitations, and no amount of study will enable him to transcend those limitations. One can discern the intellectual capacity of a person, but one can never increase that capacity any more than one can transform a talentless person into a great musician or sculptor. These considerations also apply to the capacities of different races. (SW 6 p. 663)

Language Precedes Concepts.

The child can already speak and understand his native language by the age of one, without employing concepts. Prehistoric man spoke and understood speech for untold thousands of decades without ever having utilized a single concept. It is not mankind as such, but solely *historical* mankind who announces his arrival when he discovers the first concept. Concepts could only be formulated for the first time when the meanings of words had already been established. (SW 6 pp. 657–8)

On Eugen Dühring's Contribution.

Dühring, above all other modern thinkers, is to be thanked for drawing our attention to the profound significance of the Eleatics. He is to be thanked as well for the unsurpassed clarity and sharpness of his demolition, in his *Critical History of Philosophy*, of the arguments of the Eleatics…which he achieves by means of a fundamental critique of the concept of infinity that certainly deserves the highest praise. (SW 1 p. 51)

Eros Cosmogonos.

There can be no doubt that the triumph of the spiritual and personal gods over the chthonic and elemental divinities was achieved in the Ionic cities on the hither-Asiatic seacoast long before the Greek motherland was affected. Thus, we should not hope to find in Homer any very pronounced indications regarding prehistoric religiosity. We must, in fact, seek the signs of the earlier beliefs, in part, in Hesiod, and also, in part, in the heritage of the sects and mystery-cults, which, out of the struggle of various strata of Greek religiosity, were able to precipitate the flood-tide of Dionysian worship that extended from the eighth century BCE to the sixth century…Now in Hesiod, although he scarcely mentions Eros, we certainly come upon the god, although the poet's Eros is not strictly *cosmogonos;* the Hesiodic Eros, the "most beautiful of all the immortal gods," joins Gaia and the antecedent pre-polar Chaos to constitute the primordially creative Triad out of which issue all earthly happenings. The idea of Eros as *cosmogonos* is definitively achieved in the mythic teachings of the Orphic sect; for our purposes, the most important doctrine of the Orphics tells of how Chronos, "never-aging time," fashioned the silver world-egg out of the aether and the unfathomable void. From this world-egg there emerges the shining god Phanes-Eros-Dionysos (also called Metis and Erikapaios); this is Eros the hermaphrodite divinity, the god who bears within him the seeds of all the other gods. (SW 3 p. 376)

THE BODY OF LOVE. Love may be aroused by the visible, discrete attributes or characteristics of another person: by beautiful or unique hands, feet, body-type, shape of the neck, nose, complexion, scent. The preference for blonde hair or for dark, for blue eyes or for brown, may even indicate…that the natural predilections of an individual arise, in large part, *from racial considerations.* (SW 3 p. 365)

THE DEATH OF THE EGO. The "wise man," as Goethe has told us, yearns for a death in flames, for only he understands that before the gates of life can be opened, the ego must first be slain. (SW 3 394)

FORMS OF LOVE. The "materialist" desires to possess and master man and all of man's powers. He "loves" dependability and so-called *character.*

Christ saw himself as being near the center of things; he searched for God; and his most profound yearning was that he might merge himself with "higher things." He craves the *outside* and the *up-there,* and when he loves, his sentiment is aimed in just those directions.

Eros, on the other hand, is the love of *creation.* For Eros, the boundless universe is *alive.* A flood of shimmering light breaks forth. The entire environment glows, the distance resounds: the beloved becomes a flame afar. (RR p. 264)

IMAGES. Images plunge into the mysterious darkness; they drift into a magical distance. Images are never impoverished, never permanent, never to be seized in a coarse grip; a joyous spectacle blazes up, and then it sinks into the night. (RR p. 272)

THE VEIL OF MAYA. The nineteenth century, more than any previous one, set out to tear the "Veil of Maya" asunder. With sacrilegious inquisitiveness, it probed into everything that exists: the darkness of the void, the metallic sheen of distant oceans, the wondrous song of the atmosphere, and the sublime gloom of temple and cathedral. Its reality…was merely a shield of lies behind which it concealed its lust for destruction. (RR p. 272)

THE GOLDEN AGE.

Life's gaze is always directed backwards, and where life is embodied in thought, its thought is always a contemplation of the return of vanished beings. Indeed, the collected legendry of the pagan world places all greatness, beauty, and radiance in a far-distant pre-historic world: this is the "Golden Age" of the heroic founders of noble clans. (RR p. 285)

ON THE SOUL.

The soul is the fulfilled vitality, the self-incinerating flame. That which limits and constricts itself in the waking state, becomes, in sleep, a bottomless sea.

Matter (*Hyla*) is the sleep of the soul. Its waking has the actuality of the dream: shining images glide past, and then they plunge again into the darkness.

The ocean is the symbol of the universal soul, and the ocean's phosphorescence manifests its highest vitality. Profound life blossoms only within the womb of night, and the ocean glows only nocturnally. Life is the self-rolling wheel, the *perpetuum mobile,* the mill wheel through which the waters of time must pass. (RR p. 262)

ANIMA RERUM.

Lightning is the soul of the landscape just as the shimmer is the soul of the crystal, the scent is the soul of the flower, and the eye is the soul of the animal; man is even more *eye* than is the animal, and the world in him becomes more *image.* (RR p. 263)

ROMANTICISM AND THE SOUL.

The Romantic period was wandering and exploratory, just as our own time is. Strangeness, distance, the thrill of life and the threat of storm, rapture, emotional transport, yearning for the stars: many names for the self-same essence, which is the *soul.* (RR p. 259)

THE GORGON AND THE NIGHT. There are three vital perspectives: the erotic, the heroic, and the magical. In the world of images these types are manifest as: the beloved, the hero, and the wizard. My own experience was magical (to a chaotic extreme); it was the Gorgon and the dread of universal night. I tried to approach Eros through love…But before the metallic night could extend its cloak over the house of love, love's home sank into the earthly morass. (RR p. 261)

ELEMENTAL NATURE. The elemental is not a striving towards the animal condition. It is something that is beyond man and, at the same time, close to the realm of the plants. (RR p. 261)

LENAU AND MEYER. The two most highly endowed Dionysian poets of the nineteenth century, Lenau and Conrad Ferdinand Meyer, led — one buried in his books, the other in tobacco smoke and violin music — the most secluded lives imaginable. (SW 3 p. 400)

SPIRIT AND SOUL. Only when Spirit sleeps does the soul awaken. Spirit sleeps most deeply when the senses slumber. But even in the waking state there is a sleep of the Spirit. In every act there are moments when Spirit nods and the soul opens wide its eyes. Ever richer is our life at the moments when Spirit passes through the realm of sleep. Then we are more profoundly alive, as each moment passes into the next. At such times, our eyes shine…(RR p. 264)

THE SYMBOLISM OF THE WHEEL. The polarities that constitute life were once symbolized by the wheel. We see this clearly in the myth of Ixion, where sometimes the head is above, and sometimes it is below…All of life is, in fact, polarized: we have an under and an over, a black side and a white, an ending and a beginning, and so forth. Polarities are revealed between rising and falling, between birth and death, and between the fixed and the wandering. Indeed, we may even see in the wheel the tragic symbol of the cosmogonic Eros. (RR p. 330)

THOUGHT AND IMAGE. Thought is the medium of philosophy, the handmaiden of poetry, and the elevating background of art. In the absence of thought, only the primordial image endures intact, for in the image a more profound incandescence consumes the cold light of empirical observation. The primordial images are like weighty gold or crimson enamel, whereas thoughts are like penetrating flames or lightning reflexes.

The contemporary world knows nothing of authentic images or genuine thought. Its art is without background, without atmosphere, vapid; its poetry is unfinished, harsh, arid, and destitute, or it is gaudy and absurd; and its philosophy is but an asthmatic critique. (RR p. 284)

ON THE CREATORS OF THE "FOLK SONG." For many reasons, we regard the expression "the folk song" as somewhat ambiguous, since the implication of the phrase is that its creators have been drawn exclusively from the lower classes. However, genuine folk songs have also been crafted by aristocrats and even by kings. The superb poetic ballads of Scandinavia, for instance, were largely the product of knightly and courtly circles, and these ballads are certainly authentic "folk songs!" (AC pp. 199–200)

THE WHEEL OF LIFE. Ceaselessly, the moment sinks into the past: the wheel of life is turned by death. Ceaselessly, the past darkens the purple dome of the fleeing moment: out of the realm of Hades springs the flower of Persephone. (RR p. 270)

THE EROS OF THE DISTANCE. In a mystical rotation, all that passes returns unto the night of birth. Earth drinks up the rains shed by water-born clouds, and, as the rain-drop enters the sea, so, without ceasing, dies the daylight of the present into the darkness of the past. Just as the world is girdled by the Midgard Serpent, so all that transpires is bound by the pulsating wave of the cosmic sea; and that which appears in the raging storm that hurls itself against chimney and tower outside, becomes the protective heat of the hearth-fire within. As if collected within an urn, it becomes that blood-glow of Eros that already stirs within the animal; it dreams within its blood. Unfettered, it becomes the Wild Hunt. But it is also revealed in the sweet dawning of that dazzling distance, wherein a wild darkness joins forces with alluring lamentations from afar. The crossing of gold and gloom as inseparable twilight: *Eros of the Distance*. (RR p. 271)

INNER DRIVE AND OUTER EXPRESSION. Every driving-force is at the same time a disposition of the body; and alongside every activity of a drive there occurs a physiological, *physiognomical* transformation of the body. (AC p. 16)

PARADOX. Shame is the dread that one feels before the prospect of one's true *self* being exposed. Thus, shame is, without a doubt, to be classed with those emotions that are ordinarily called *egotistical*. (AC p. 17)

THE WISE MAN AND HIS WISDOM. No sage has ever lived his life according to his wisdom: in the truly wise man, his wisdom is the philosophical *expression* of his life. What we call "self-mastery" is always but one specific mode of the momentary preponderance of a single impulse. Obviously, there can be no authentic mastery over our passions, any more than there can be a genuine "freedom of the will." (AC p. 17)

ON CRUELTY. Cruelty belongs to the most "forbidden" elements of the affective life. We can scarcely pronounce the word *cruelty* without arousing in the listener a dark, and therefore so much more intensely felt, loathing for that train of phantoms that our long religious training of the heart has clothed with flesh and blood. (We can best clarify our thoughts regarding these difficult matters by consulting the works of the great German thinkers of the nineteenth century.)

But as to how matters stand in the real world, we must understand that the yearning for violence and suffering belongs not to "man in general," but solely to historical man. Let us recall — without veiling the eyes, if you please — the gladiatorial combat of the Romans, the naïve maliciousness of so many children, and the Spaniard's delight in the bull-fight. In addition, however, we must not ignore the ingredient of cruelty in the pleasure that people derive from attending a great theatrical tragedy; in the breathless anticipation with which many people listen to chronicles of atrocities that transpired in far distant ages and cultures; in the love of scandal and gossip; in the everyday amusement that some experience in the misfortunes of others; in truculence and "braggadocio"; in the longing to make an "impression" on the world; and in the great delight that so many people take in witnessing the downfall and disgrace of their fellow man. (AC pp. 17–18)

Christian Lust for Self-Torture. The major achieve-

ment of Christianity was in relocating the arena within which man conducts his operations from the world outside of man to the landscape of the human soul within…The admitted cruelty of the ancient world was then forced to don the guise of the contrite penitent. Antiquity took what was perhaps an excessive pleasure in battle and death; but the self-same lust has characterized the entire Christian era as well, although the Christian has sought to hide his suicidal impulses behind such masks as *self-flagellation* and *asceticism*. (AC p. 18)

Truth-Criterion. Throughout the ages many thinkers have

attempted to answer the nagging question regarding the criterion for determining truth; but the problem can never be solved adequately, as any answer would presuppose the truth of the procedure whereby the problem had been solved!

There are also, however, occasions when such quests for a truth-criterion are unnecessary, since there are several propositions, both factual and philosophical, that we are told are universally compelling ("immediately evident"). On the other hand, it is important that we bear in mind that the predicates "true" and "false" pertain solely to our judgments. In the absence of a thinking consciousness, truth and error simply cannot exist. (SW 3 720)

JUDGMENT AND WORLD. Our critical judgment cannot perceive red, blue, or any color whatsoever *in general;* nor can our judgment perceive sounds, tastes, musical key-signatures, thirst or hunger *in themselves;* our judgment cannot perceive discrete feelings of hope, yearning, expectation, and so on. What our judgments of the world can achieve is this: the perception of the manifold of qualities, both internal and external, that enable us to distinguish one thing from another. (SW 3 P. 721)

BACK TO THE ROMANTICS! We live in an age when empirical science and its monuments are overrated. A mere knowledge of the facts in the case now passes for something substantial. Certainly, a well-founded science should perform its operations with the aid of just such facts as are necessary to prove its theories. Everything else is useless ballast. Originally, this method was fitting and proper when considered against the background of a reaction against the debauchery of the *Naturphilosophie* of the early nineteenth century. But today there is no longer any need for such a negative viewpoint. The ceaseless defamation of speculative ideas now permits fashionable writers to ignore even the *uncontested* advances that Schelling, Oken, and others contributed to the advancement of science. It is high time that we recall the achievements of the Romantics, so that we may cease traveling down the path of an obtuse "induction." (LK GL p. 147)

SCIENCE AND METAPHYSICS. Science is not a matter of collecting facts, but of asking the right questions. The history of science demonstrates this quite clearly. It also shows that the truly great discoverers always achieved their crucial results with the aid of speculation (the data upon which they based their theories was often quite limited)…Think of a Dalton, of a Robert Mayer, of an Avogadro. These are the three great names of their age in our own field of study, and all three strikingly bear out the truth of our contention. And, *nota bene,* all three were forced to live their creative lives in mortal combat with their contemporaries! (LK GL p. 148)

FROM "MANLY LOYALTY" TO "HOMOSEXUALITY." The attempt to saturate the *sexual* instinct with the *erotic* essence has often resulted in the downfall of the lovers; on the other hand, the contrary attempt — to sever the instinct from the essence — has led and still leads initially to the poisoning of Eros, and ultimately to its death. Here we must emphasize the fact that displays of sympathy are oftentimes more profound between members of the same sex than between man and woman. The eternal icon here is the Dioscuri [the mythological twins Castor and Pollux]; this sympathetic bond celebrates its highest festival in honoring friendship as much as it honors affection...When we recall the "manly loyalty" of the ancient Germans, we also summon to our mind's eye the original "manly affection" of the ancient Greeks, which likewise had scarcely anything in common with contemporary "homosexuality." The Greek sentiment first began to degenerate as a result of the evil entanglement of the impulse to heterosexual union with a banal love of boys...The Eros of the West stands under the sign of "Blood-brotherhood," of which the "sacred league" of the Thebans is perhaps the best world-historical example. (SW 3 pp. 406–7)

NATURE AND SOUL. In spite of all of the idle chatter about "progress," there are still prophetic souls who draw our attention to the implications of the indubitable increase of man's mastery (alas! along with man's destruction) of nature. But even these prophets have not devoted sufficient attention to the simultaneous and equally blatant assaults on the *values of the soul!* (SW 3 p. 654)

FROM THINGS TO IMAGES. Although to our human senses it might seem to be merely a promise of bliss, we receive much more when we drink our fill from the beaker that is offered to us by the *Eros of the distance*, which releases us from the tangible world of things, and transports us to the ungraspable *actuality of the images!* (SW 3 p. 412)

BACK TO THE PRE-SOCRATICS! The student who immerses himself, lovingly and intelligently, in the symbolic language of the pre-Socratics, must unfailingly conclude that no succeeding age — and especially not that of the pretentious twin peaks of Hellenic wisdom, Plato and Aristotle! — has matched the profundity and panoramic scope of those dazzling philosophical ruins that we continually visit in our quest for wisdom: Thales, Anaximander, Heraclitus, Empedocles, and Pythagoras are their names. The least that can be said of these giants is that they were well on the way to the discovery that an authentic interpretation of the world must entail a *doctrine of life*. They also understood that the *mechanistic* aspect of reality should be reduced to the status of an insignificant by-product of the living world. (SW 3 p. 654)

IN A NUTSHELL. Our position is that the primal *Trias,* from which every authentic triad has descended, ordains that body and soul are the poles of life; into the substance of man — more precisely, into man as he rides the wave-crest of "World History" — there possibly erupts a force from outside the spatio-temporal realm (acosmic). That force is named *Spirit,* and Spirit's mission is to sever the poles of body and soul and thereby to murder the living substance of man. (SW 3 p. 565)

TERMINUS. The spiritual will to conquest is the ultimate offense against life, and the offender must be prepared to endure life's harsh retaliation in consequence. This proposition will remain in force so long as mankind exists, and it will have demonstrated the full horror of its ultimate implications when a degenerate mankind finally evolves into a completely rationalized and desecrated counterfeit of life. (SW 3 p. 479)

SEX AND EROS. We can liken sex to the harsh light of a glowing electric wire. Eros, however, is more like the intense and frosty shimmer of opalescent glass...Erotic vitality resembles an elegant lamp that discharges its radiance symmetrically throughout one's entire study. (SW 3 p. 490)

GOD AS SUICIDE. For two thousand years the Christian religion, with its hatred of the world, has found its symbol of life in the self-cruci-fixion of the creator of that world! (SW 3 p. 481)

THE GREAT ACHIEVEMENT. It was Aristotle who first realized that the pure, i.e., functioning — albeit not suffering — Spirit (*nous*) is an entity that has erupted into the cosmos from *outside* the cosmos: we en-dorse this formulation. (SW 3 p. 736)

ACTUALITY AND EXPERIENCE. Actuality is experienced, but truth is thought that is based upon experience. That which we contem-plate conceptually is not actuality; but the conceptual dimension can aid us in our efforts to comprehend that actuality. (SW 3 589)

THE MYSTIC AND THE EROS OF THE DISTANCE. Human drives are blessed by Eros to the extent that they participate in the cosmic Eros; and cosmic Eros is always: *Eros of the distance*. Thus, whoever seeks to negate distance is characterized by a possessiveness that is fatal to Eros, to the glowing *nimbus* of the world, and, ultimately, to actuality itself.

Nevertheless, the real secret endures, as does the sacred wisdom of the mystic: the holy image is only revealed from afar, even as the mystic merges himself with his vision. The mystic alone sees "the sun aglow at midnight." (SW 3 p. 482)

ABOVE AND BELOW. The necessary counterpart of "salvation in heaven" is hell on earth. (SW 3 p. 468)

IMAGE AND SYMBOL. The actuality of the image — the most in-tense (perhaps the only!) actuality to which we have access — is an eter-nal coming to be and passing away, a perpetual waxing and waning, the kindling as well as the extinguishing of the light. In sharp contrast to the time-bound rigidity of modern existence, the actuality of the image can-not be trapped in concepts. Instead, it communicates more and evermore to us through the language of the *symbol*. (SW 3 p. 469)

THE ETIOLOGY OF "HUMANITARIANISM." Starting out from the time when a combative chorus of voices strove to determine who should rule the heathen tribes during the Germanic migrations, we end up today with the exaggeratedly sympathetic nature of the Nordic race, which we have to thank for the disastrous gift of a syrupy "soul love" (as confusing and fatal as any gift could possibly be: because the combative chorus of the heathens degenerated through the collapse of *the capacity to discriminate;* then it became the perfectly achieved, universally tolerant *harmonization.* Tempted by Christian catchphrases, that tolerance became, in turn, *exclusive passion,* about which we still hear so much today. Ultimately, "soul love" transformed its substance into the destructive specter of universal "humanitarianism," which is, in fact, *the murderer of love*). (SW 3 p. 404)

MONIST AND DUALIST. Whether we hold with the materialists that the ultimately "real" substances are atoms, or electrons, or protons; or with the idealists that the truly real is mere "being," Spirit (*logos*), reason (*nous*), the "absolute," or the transcendental place that houses ideas or non-extensible monads, etc.: all of these viewpoints agree in situating the "real" beyond the world of phenomenal *images,* in comparison with which all of those candidates fade into oblivion. And it is no different in the merely apparent opposition of "dualism" and "monism," since behind the former's "duality" there always lurks a pure "one," to which, at the end of the day, even the "dualist" feels compelled to grant the status of the ultimately "real." (SW 3 736)

PSEUDO-PSYCHOLOGISTS. Although they call themselves psychologists, our academics appear to us to be, in fact, *epistemologists,* for it is immediately apparent that their researches consistently deal with such matters as feelings, perceptions, representations, etc. They never seem to have pondered the fact that it is not consciousness alone — and without certain presuppositions regarding consciousness, all of their systems would immediately crumble to dust — but the "activity of the senses" as well that is subject to periodic alternations between existence and non-existence. They speak so dispassionately about a "stream of conscious-ness" where they should be studying the stream of *life*; what's more, many of them are intrepid enough to draw the inexorable conclusion that there is a stream of *sleep*-consciousness as well.

Everyone laughs and considers himself entitled to ridicule as mere sophistries the doctrines of the Eleatics, who held that events were "de-ceptive illusions." But even serious thinkers today advance the view that perhaps our sleep-consciousness also merits the name of conscious-ness, without realizing that they have thereby plunged themselves into a counterpart of the Eleatics' error. The Eleatics disavowed the continuity of events, on the grounds that this continuity was conceptually unten-able (by reason of the discontinuity of comprehension); the other school affirms the continuity of consciousness inasmuch as, without it, one would be unable conceptually to grasp the continuity of events. Thus, one school avoids contact with actuality, while the other is divorced from the *experience* of actuality; fundamentally, however, both schools are united in assenting to the proposition that consciousness alone is the "true" real-ity! (SW 2 p. 804)

DREAM AND PAIN. The dream-experience is an experience that is not susceptible to suffering. (SW 2 p. 809)

VITAL RHYTHM. The rhythm of life undoubtedly differs between one person and another; this is even more the case when we examine different races and species. (SW 2 p. 825)

BEFORE THE ALTAR OF THE PELASGIANS. The illustrious historian Herodotus tells us that at Dodona he learned that the original inhabitants of Hellas, who were called the "Pelasgians," had certainly hon-ored the gods and offered sacrifices to them, but they did not know their names, which were only later discovered by the Egyptians. After these divine names were recognized by the Oracle at Dodona, they were in due course transmitted to the Hellenes. What is the deeper implication of this account of Herodotus? Consider the following: for the Pelasgians, as for any similar people in the primordial phase of cultural development, all of the following entities possessed a sacred character—heaven, earth, the sea, the stream, the mountain, the tree, the soil, the animal, the stone, the rustling of the treetop, the moaning of the wind, the passing cloud, light and darkness, the fructifying rain, burning passion, sun and moon, the orbit of the star, the arrival of the seasons, morning and evening, brightness and darkness, the house, the herd, the kindling of the flame, the livestock and the harvest, the bath, drinking and eating, the nuptial feast, pregnancy and birth, the bond between parents and their children, dying, sleeping, dreaming, quarrel and atonement, promise and betrayal, coming to be and passing away, melancholy and joy, welfare and misfortune, longing and loathing, the blessing and the curse, guilt and revenge, health and sickness, high spirits, madness, and so very much more! (SW 5 p. 371)

ON THE ONTOLOGICAL SCHOOL. If the ontological school had been relentlessly serious in its attempt to develop a *logic without a subject,* then ontology itself, if we do not err, would have perished in the very hour of its birth! (SW 5 p. 369)

THE KEY TO SPIRIT. In our metaphysics, we separate the life-cell from the *Spirit*—that power from outside the world—and, with Nietzsche, we find the key to the nature of Spirit not in the intellect, but in the *will.* (PEN p. 144)

GOETHE ON PASSION. Goethe has no rival as the poet of passion and passionate love; but he permits his disciples of passion, almost without exception, to experience a tragic downfall: recall Werther, Clavigo, Eduard, Ottilie, Egmont, Tasso, Faust, Gretchen, Weislingen, and so on. He never wearies of assuring his readers that limitless passion results in misfortune. (SW 5 p. 228)

THE FOOLISHNESS OF "PANTHEISM." Pantheism, taken as literally as so many people appear to take it, is certainly the most idiotic of all the "isms" that have ever been concocted. According to this doctrine, the greatness of heroes is divine, the lying of the hypocrite is divine, the treachery of the plotter is divine, the malice of the slanderer is divine, the scent of the rose is divine, and even the stench of acetylene is divine! Now if the pantheist is utilizing such terms as "God," "Godhead," and "Godliness" as mere synonyms for *being,* then he would be well-advised to come right out and say so! (SW 5 p. 228)

THOUGHT AND WISDOM. The oldest wisdom of mankind was the possession and sole prerogative of woman, as we can see from the tales of the Pythia, the Sibyls, the priestesses of Ida, the swan-maidens, and the Valkyries. That which the unique disposition of woman has contributed to our attempts to discover wisdom is betrayed even now in the expression "mother wit" [*Mutterwitz*]. The exaggeratedly masculine West created a culture of *thought,* whereas the more feminine Asian world (China especially) gave birth to a culture of *wisdom,* whose most delicate bloom is Taoism. SW 5 pp. 221–2)

THE "MYSTERIOUS ROAD." When Novalis contemplated the unique research conducted by the Romantics (which proceeded along the same lines as the research of Goethe, but which also went beyond it), and pronounced the strangely Sibyline sentence: "The mysterious road leads inward," he did not mean to say that, like someone staring at his own navel, we should focus our gaze upon our own person and away from the phenomenal world. He did mean to say that only through devotion to the world of images could the eye of Spirit be opened, whereby it could perceive amid the appearances the soul to whom they appear; and in the same way it could perceive in the outer world the inner life that expresses its ever-changing vitality there. (SW 5 p. 234)

TONES AND NOISES. The science of acoustics treats of tones and tonal combinations; but in reality we never truly hear tones, but exclusively noises, since even the pure tone of the tuning fork can only strike the ear as does any other noise. Thus, language has no precise notation-system whereby it can denote *tone-qualities in general,* although language is indeed able to differentiate between innumerable *noises:* howling, rolling, roaring, booming, thundering, bellowing, cracking, clattering…and so forth. (SW 1 p. 180)

IMAGE AND THING. The perceived image…constitutes an event; the thing figures in the event, but only as the unchanging fragment of duration inhering in that event. (SW 1 p. 181)

TIME AND SPACE, IMAGES AND THINGS. Events are species of happenings, and all happenings entail a spatio-temporal aspect. In the perceived image, whether it is seething and hissing, or only a fixed, linear array, the image comes to us as an immediately present spatio-temporal actuality, in which space and time are the connected poles, indivisible and without location, formed but without limit. Before things comes to us, on the other hand, space and time must be mediated by the connectedness of extra-spatio-temporal points existing in-themselves and for-themselves [*an und fuer sich*]. (SW 1 p. 181)

DEAD THINGS, LIVING POWERS. In the world of things, whatever is moved necessarily receives that movement from without; thus, the thing is never self-moved. This insight may provide a hint as to why physics neglects, as it must, a consideration of the distinction between *activity* and *passivity* (just as geometry omits the distinction between right and left).

"Powers," on the other hand, initiate movement from within. Only they can act; only they can suffer. (SW p. 187)

KNOWLEDGE AND MORTALITY. The consciousness of existence is one and the same with consciousness of *mortality.* We can acquire foreknowledge, but we can only purchase it at the price of our conscious anticipation of death. (SW 1 p. 448)

FORMALISM AND SUBSTANTIALISM. Formalism rules physics, just as it rules the human sciences. The apparent successes that formalism can display have more or less enabled it to drive true science out of many areas of research. But formalism is debarred from one particular field: that of psychology and characterology! Here in fact we must walk upon the soil of experience. One can *expel* experience from formalistic thought, but formalistic thought cannot *interpret* experience!

Two types of thinking thus stand in an attitude of mortal enmity: the *formalistic* type, which claims to celebrate its supreme triumphs in mathematics — and *finance;* and *substantial* thought, which is on the verge of extinction, and which has its homeland, so to speak, in — *the soul.* Thus, I am one of the "last Mohicans" of substantial thought; [Melchior] Palagyi sought to introduce substantialism into physics; the attempt was doomed to failure. Physics will die — after the final paroxysms of technology — and it will die at the hands of relativistic formalism. (LK GL p. 1105)

THE DEATH OF GERMANY (FROM A LETTER WRITTEN IN 1947). An evil star reigns over this year. A great shadow has darkened my world since I learned on January 23 of the death of my beloved sister, a death that was her final release from dreadful suffering. Her loss has been unendurable, and I see her death almost as an impersonal and tragic symbol of my dying homeland. Both of us had requested permission to say our sad farewells in person, since we both knew that delay would be fatal. In vain! The Allies are granting passports only to industrialists, known collaborators, and, finally, to those creatures who, in lieu of visas, brandish the slanderous diatribes that they have written against Germany. (LK GL pp. 1361–2)

ON WILL AS SERVANT OF LIFE. The expressive potential in the formative movements of talented individuals is in sharp contrast with what we find in the merely mechanical movements of the willful, in whom Spirit has released itself from its connection with the soul; and the expressive movements of the talented also differ from the restless, rhythmical motions that we find in primitive peoples, in that the talented individuals have been able masterfully to press the will into the service of life, so that even in the historical phase, the "head" spontaneously avows its adherence to the "heart," to the extent that it is energized by the pulsation of the heart. (SW 6 pp. 654–5)

ON EXPRESSION-RESEARCH [AUSDRUCKSKUNDE].

Expression-Research is the scientific discipline that investigates the psychical content [*vom seelischen Gehalt*] of the functional transformations occurring in the bodily constitution of man and animal. Among such transformations we have: the acceleration and the retardation of pulsatory and respiratory movements, the prolongation or the shortening of the pulse rate and respiratory rate, the dilation and contraction of the pupils, changes in digestion, muscular spasms, the emission of sweat, and so on. Many of these phenomena can be satisfactorily investigated only within the controlled conditions of the experimental laboratory; others are readily visible in normal environments. Among the latter we have changes in pulse and respiration, blushing and becoming pale, and so on. Among the most visible and, therefore, the most easily dealt with conceptually, are the involuntary expressive movements. Basically, these movements pervade the entire body (along with other functional alterations). Joyous excitement can find expression in such phenomena as: the acceleration of the gait, the liveliness of the gestures, the raising of the voice, the lifting of the head, the easing of the facial musculature, the heightened gleam in the eyes, an elevated redness of the complexion (resulting from the distention of the blood-vessels), and so on. Then we have the contrasting group of expressions that accompany the condition of sadness (the relaxation of the muscles, bowed posture, the retardation of movement in general, increased pallor, and so on). Above all, this science has turned its attentions to the investigation of the expressive movements associated with the *sentiments* (rages, affects, emotions).

Among the host of researchers who were involved in expression-research in the latter half of the nineteenth century (Duchenne, Gratiolet, Spencer, Bell, Mosso, Lehmann, Wundt, Lange, James), the two towering figures are Darwin and Piderit. It was Darwin who first established the essential equivalence of emotional expression in all of the human races, by means of an ingeniously designed questionnaire, which he distributed to thirty-six explorers, colonial officials, missionaries, etc. In addition, through careful observation of the behavior of a multitude of animals, Darwin demonstrated — at the very least — the comprehensive similarity that exists even between the expressive movements of man and those of the animal. He was, unfortunately, less successful in his theoretical forays. Here, Piderit was more effective, although he limited his investigations to the study of facial mimicry. These studies anticipated the most recent work in the field, which goes beyond an analysis of merely transitory conditions in order to arrive at a comprehensive study of the organism that produces the expressive movement. In our own publications, the author of these lines has transformed expression-theory into a comprehensive *physiognomics* of functional transformations. (SW 6 pp. 687–8)

THE SYMPHONIC RHYTHMS OF EARTH. Whoever attends to the great symphony of rhythms, sooner or later has occasion to observe that organic and cosmic tides constitute polarized forms of a rhythmical totality that corresponds to rhythms that occur in both the organic and the super-organic realms. At the very least we can affirm that our earth stands under the sign of *an enduring pulsation.* We think of the rhythm (never regular!) of the melting of winter's snow, of the annual rhythm of rising and falling rivers, of the rhythm of commingling waters as springs pour forth their floods, of the rainy seasons in tropical regions, of the periodic fluctuation in the depth of the water-table, of the day-to-day periodicity of atmospheric pressure, temperature, humidity, and electrical conductivity, of the daily, yearly, and centennial rhythms of magnetic declination and inclination, of the monthly, biannual, and yearly periodicity of the polar aurora, of the periodicity of windless "doldrums," and so on. When we consider the rhythms in *forms*, it is impossible to ignore the fact that the rhythm (never regular!) of the oceanic tides provides an apt paradigm for a whole host of telluric formations. We recall sand dunes (both consolidated and shifting), the oceanic interior of continental deserts, the wave-like patterns formed by cirrus clouds, the wave-crests of mountain and mountain-chain.

Typical plant-forms recur in certain classes of animals as they do in the contours of the earth itself. Who can be unaware of the similarities between the rhythmical branching of the tree and the ramifying of the great river networks, or the tree-like ramification of the human nerve-centers! (SW 2 p. 827)

FALSE PHILOSOPHERS. Restless, rambling, enthusiastic spirits invariably lack the slightest trace of a profound originality. Their speculations either degenerate into a hollow species of rationalism, or they lead to a superficial game of wits that is played out with phantoms in which even they do not seriously believe.

From Plato to Hegel, the entire host of so-called philosophers can be divided into two camps: first, we have those half-sober, and therefore uncritical, phantom-mongers; and second, we have these arrogant hyper-rationalists, i.e., such fellows as are shallow enough to convince themselves that life is a rational phenomenon! (RR p. 346)

THE TWO STYLES OF ART. When we avert our gaze from the almost demonic primitive modes of art (Egyptian, Assyrian, Aztec, Peruvian, and primitive), we realize that for us there are really only two types of art: the Apollonian-Ancient and the Gothic-Germanic. The first signifies the road to the *appearances*, while the second marches down the road to *actions*. (RR p. 329)

LOSS OF MEANING. How will we ever be able to elicit the full content of words that we can no longer really comprehend, such as the "will" of Schopenhauer, the "absolute" and the "infinite" of Schelling, the "a priori" of Kant, and the "pneuma" of the Gnostics?! In the strictest sense, philosophy has as little chance of being translated out of its tongue and its time as poetry has. (RR p. 365)

THE FAITH IN THE IMAGES. We have access to countless examples of the faith in the images as it existed during prehistory in the surviving emblematic forms of non-conceptual, symbolic thought. We are able to arrange in a chronological series a great range of evidence: from the sagas and faiths, from the fetishes and magical practices, from the soothsaying and the superstitions, from sacred customs and celebrations, and, in brief, from the entire heritage of prehistory, to demonstrate the fact that life-bound Spirit's limitless creative variety — both in the degenerate and falling and in the healthy and perfect — is based upon the rule of the faith in images over the faith in the actuality of things; and this irrefutable fact enables us to understand, with a certitude that is beyond the reach of discursive consciousness, the following fundamental truths: the essential unity of the images with the active powers of the world in general; the essential unity of the images with each other according to the measure of their elementary similarities; the essential unity of specific images with their symbolic signs; and, finally, the essential unity of the *image-receiving* with the *symbol-imparting,* soul of man. (SW 2 pp. 1257–8)

ETERNALLY VALID. The soulless lust for power of Rome was massively amplified by the surreptitious addition of the Jewish lust for power, and henceforth these two have magnified the empire of the papacy: *The papacy is nothing but Judaized Caesarism.* (SW 2 p. 1243)

THE BODY-SOUL UNITY. Just as the soul is the formative principle of the living body, so is the living body the phenomenon and revelation of the soul. (AC p. 304)

FROM HEROISM TO MODERNITY. The fate that befell the Indo-Europeans can immediately be comprehended when we look at the four "epic" peoples: the Indians, the Persians, the Greeks, and the Germans. In all of these cultures, the vital activity bifurcates into two forms of expression, i.e., the heroic and the poetic...Both were and are possible without the will to power, and the participation of these "epic" peoples in both modes of expression is recalled in the bloody battlefields filled with the shining deeds of heroic, self-sacrificing warriors, as well as in their artistic creations that are still bathed in the light of their poetic immortality.

But when the Indo-Europeans fell into the clutches of Spirit, heroism degenerated into rationalism and technology. The Anglo-Saxon peoples stood in the vanguard of this disastrous development. Its pinnacle is reached in today's Americanism.

Even among the Semites there was a people whose essential soul reveals certain affinities with the soul of the Indo-European: the Arabs, who, in certain limited areas, can be said to stand in polar contrast to the Indo-European peoples. Just as one can compare the Viking essence to the surge of the storm-tormented North Sea, one can similarly compare the essence of the Islamic Arab to a desert storm. Who knows whether Spain could have functioned as the connecting link in that wondrous synthesis of Eastern and Western actuality that the great Friedrich II Hohenstaufen had in mind, had Spain not already tied herself to that revolution which Nietzsche called the victorious "slave revolt in morality," which was brought about by the instilling of the Spirit of Yahwistic Judaism in all the downtrodden dregs of the Roman Empire? The Jew Saul — "St. Paul" — made the great advance when he made the world safe for his beloved "Spirit." And the Spirit of Pauline Judaism is still around today, although it calls itself — *Christendom*. (SW 2 p. 1242)

ROME AND POWER. No one will dispute the greatness of the history of Rome. The inferiority of Rome to Greece in heroism and poetry can only be matched by Rome's superiority in her unbridled will to power. (SW 2 pp. 1242–3)

THE WEST I. We can only understand alien races when we take the Germanic nature as normative; this direction of apprehension cannot be reversed.

The Oriental soul manifests a sickly exaltation and has nothing whatever in common with the force of soul that radiates from the audacious and mild luster of Germanic eyes.

Even the Greek soul differs from the Germanic. The Greek soul is weaker, more southern, more hermaphroditic, and more plastic. The Germanic soul is bolder, more Nordic, more masculine, more wandering, more profound, and more *cosmic*. Beauty has a more difficult birth in the Germanic realm than it has in the Greek, but the content housed in Germanic beauty is far more powerful. (RR p. 249)

THE WEST II. A profound abyss yawns between the priestly races and the heroic ones; the noble races also pray, but only to their heroes. Demonic powers inhabit these gigantic warriors, who scorn the spiritual devotion of the Catholic saints. The Aryans who conquered ancient India sprang from a heroic, primordial race, whereas the sanctity of the Indian priests originated in a purely Asiatic, "peasant" spirituality. But *every* peasantry is obviously gentler than an adventurous aristocracy. (RR p. 251)

THE SYRIAN INFECTION. Even before the advent of Christianity, the Romans had already succumbed to Stoicism, whose springs also arose in Syria. (RR p. 251)

THE WESTERN NATURE. In the East, in the South, and also in the world of antiquity, color, light, "form," and vision rule the scene; in the western Germanic world, it is moderation, sound, and pleasing scents. The dense texture of actuality in its greatest breadth is also "Western." Its essence is heavier, harder, more metallic, and, in the work area, it is more pitiless, more *formed,* and more enduring. The hardness of the North is the hardness of metal, i.e., a *supple* hardness. The *Southeast* has conquered us, however; and we still have not given birth to our authentic essence. (RR p. 311)

ON MASTERS. The master has the power; he doesn't have to seek it out. He binds and even alters the stream of power solely in the interests of *life*. (RR p. 293)

SYMBOLISM. The unity of life is not individual, it is divine. It was only in later times that the gods first assumed the guise of individuals. This is made obvious in the allegorical interpretations concocted by an already partially mechanized mankind. The primordial microcosmic symbol is the *swastika;* animal symbols are also microcosmic. However, trees, monoliths, pyramids, sphinxes, and prehistoric gravesites are all macrocosmic. (RR p. 317)

POLITICS. Among the pagans, only the Romans were able to develop the grand style in politics, and Rome perished because Roman politics, like the politics of our own age, finally succumbed to the contagion of *Judea.* And Judea's politics is now the politics of the whole world. (RR p. 322)

ACTUALITIES. That there are for us two actualities, one of customary consciousness and one of the soul, is the philosophical expression of the cleft in our inner being, which entered the sphere of life with Plato and Christ. (RR p. 475)

IN THE "YEAR OF SALVATION." The most impudent Jewish attempt to blot out the prehistoric world succeeded when Christianity identified the birth year of its founder with the birth-year of *time itself.* (RR p. 349)

ON CHARACTEROLOGY [CHARAKTERKUNDE]. Two basic modes of psychology have co-existed alongside each other for quite some time: one type of "psychology" devotes its energies to the investigation of the facts of consciousness; whereas the other school of thought investigates the nature of the whole *personality;* the latter discipline first received its designation as "Characterology" during the nineteenth century. There is a wealth of material to be discovered in the poets, sages, and moralists of the ages that has only been systematically worked over in recent years. We especially recall the pronouncements of Democritus and those of the more important Greek Sophists, as well as the contributions of the later Stoics, most especially those of Seneca, Marcus Aurelius, and Epictetus. Then we have Theophrastus, a student and disciple of Aristotle, who, in his renowned "Ethical Characters," presented a series of fragmentary analyses of thirty character-types; unfortunately, the acumen of Theophrastus is seriously impaired as a result of his attending to the sirensong of his *consistency-mania.* This work was translated into French in the seventeenth century by La Bruyere, who himself published an outstanding treatise entitled *Characters.* We also recall the French moralists and skeptics who flourished during the sixteenth and seventeenth centuries: Montaigne, Pascal, and, above all, de Rochefoucauld, the author of the dazzling *Maxims.* The problems of characterology first came into view in Germany during the intellectual Renaissance of our classical age. Goethe's *Elective Affinities* and, above all, Jean Paul's *Levana* both provide unsurpassed treasures of the greatest interest for the characterologist. Likewise, there were many useful characterological observations in the *Aphorisms* of Lichtenberg, and even the prominent epistemologist Immanuel Kant discussed the foundations of characterology in his *Anthropology.* The investigations of these students soon intersected with the physiognomical studies of Lavater, Camper, and Gall; the soil was thus well prepared for the biocentric psychology of the German Romantics. Towering above them all, is the recently re-discovered late Romantic physician Carl Gustav Carus, whose masterworks are the *Psyche: On the Developmental History of the Soul* and the *Symbolism of the Human Anatomy.* There are many worthwhile discoveries to be found as well in the works of Arthur Schopenhauer. From Schopenhauer the thread of tradition leads directly to the philosopher and pedagogue Julius Bahnsen, who brought out his two-volume treatise, the *Contributions to Characterology*, in 1867, in which the learned author first gives the illustrious child its proper name. After Bahnsen's time, however, the thread of the characterological tradition was snapped.

Eventually, the pre-dominant natural-scientific, "experimental" psychology drove the science of character almost completely from the field. Works by French students, such as the *Characters* by Paulhan, and the *Temperament and Character* by Fouillee, remained without influence. One began to hear on all sides that a complete revolution in psychology was at hand.

At that time, it was customary to demand that psychology furnish the correct instructions to employers regarding the suitability of job-applicants for specific vocations. Under the pressure of this demand, a field of research was developed which devoted itself to the study of human aptitudes and "Psychotechnics" (Muensterberg, Stern, Meumann, and others). Thereupon characterology began to penetrate psychiatry. The results of the investigations undertaken in this area by neurologists, for the most part in close conjunction with "psychoanalysts," are still somewhat murky.

But now, a powerful revolution really did break out, a revolution that had its origins in the psychological doctrines of the philosopher Friedrich Nietzsche. Basing itself firmly upon these doctrines, there soon appeared — under the illustrious name that Bahnsen had first bestowed upon the science — the first modern, systematic treatise on characterology, which was published by the author of these lines in 1910, under the title *The Principles of Characterology*. The doctrines propounded in this concise, but epoch-making work, for the first time established, as they will continue to determine, the future direction of characterology. (SW 4 pp. 708–9)

ON HYSTERIA AND SANCTITY.

Imitation is the common characteristic of all hysterical phenomena. When we read reports concerning the monks and nuns of the Middle Ages who were declared blessed, or saints (most especially if we read their own accounts!), we are amazed at the startling similarity of the ecstasies that are recounted, and at the grotesque lack of mythopoeic imagination that characterizes these stories. Thus, regarding the phenomenon of stigmatization, over and over again we encounter the following: the Christ appears, either in the guise of a child, or as the crucified adult, and he offers the choice of a floral crown or a crown of thorns; of course, the latter is chosen. The Christ then touches the region of the heart with a rod, a spear, or a beam of light (in order to mark the lateral wound). Later, he will grant the full stigmata, with its familiar five rays that emanate from the lateral wound, the hands, and the feet. The rays may be blood-red or they may be a dazzling white. The impression of the wounds will reach its high point on Good Friday. In brief, the same series of phantoms arrives on cue, and is repeated, over and over again, always in strictest obedience to the scriptural authorities established by the church.

Further, the types of phenomena that occur in eras that were stirred unto their very depths (which are merely the incubation periods of the mechanism of hysteria) throw light, not so much on this mechanism as on the condition, based on racial history, of its origins. These "saints" will to resemble their savior as closely as possible, just as they wish to enjoy all of his sufferings. Above all, they will desire to be tortured by him. But such instances of willing could never produce the internal image unless that, of which the willing is but a conscious symptom, had already occurred in the person's vital stratum, i.e., as an internal cleavage, or schism, which thenceforth we can examine very conveniently in its conscious results. Why do the saints desire to suffer such torments and pains? Because they wish to punish the body, because they wish to mount an extreme resistance to its requirements, to its claims, and to its desires. Let us now consider the significance of these facts.

Every living being is a totality possessing two poles, body and soul: body the manifestation of soul, and soul the meaning of the manifested body. The movements (in part locomotor and in part formative) constitute expressions, urges, and intuitions of that which is expressed in them. The crucial experience of the body is sensual pleasure, the central experience of the soul the joy of exultant creativity. The pre-condition for the highest development of the body, as well as of the soul, can only be maintained in the equipoise of these two poles. To wage war against the body entails making war upon such joy, and to wage war against such joy also means to expel the soul and leave it homeless, to drain its creative enthusiasm, to dry up the springs of creativity. But why do these saints wish to wage war against the body? Why do they crave (at least unintentionally) that which is the inevitable consequence: to expel the soul, to extirpate creative exaltation, to paralyze creativity? It is because the soul was sundered by the a-cosmic power of Spirit (*logos, pneuma, nous*), whose very essence is will, the adversary and murderer of life. Either one understands this, and then the supernatural visions, the examples of demonic possession, the hysteria, and, finally, personality itself, are understood; or else one cannot understand all this, and nothing at all will result but additional confusion of speech by means of that Tower of Babel of emergency concepts that dire need constrains us to erect as a substitute for thought. A hundred attempts have been made to derive the repression of body and life from life itself, but all such attempts are more blind than would be the attempt to demonstrate of the flame that is extinguished by pouring water upon it that the flame has extinguished itself by transforming a part of itself into the water that is being utilized to extinguish it! (SW 4 pp. 333–4)

THE CRUCIFIXION OF SOUL AND BODY. The mankind of heathen temples and festivals, of Gothic cathedrals and shining twilights, of pomp and circumstance and organ-tones, is finished, yielding place to a generation that reveals itself in the Stock Exchange, radio, airplane, telephone, movies, factories, poison gas, precision instruments, and newspapers. The pilgrim's path has its stations, but all of them end up at Golgotha. Similarly, the story of Spirit in Europe has its crucial chapters, which announce themselves as follows: the war of body and soul, dis-embodiment of the soul, or condemnation of joy, or paralysis of creative force; extinction of the soul in the body, or the blinding of intuition, or the body as machine; and man as the instrument of the will to power, which replaces the soul with soul-mimicry, phantoms, and masks. (SW 4 p. 336)

THE BLOOD-GLOW AND THE DEMONIC POWERS. The blood-glow ([Alfred] Schuler) is an uninterrupted, profoundly disturbing access of *awe*. A dark atmosphere throbs and ferments within hidden hovels. Wild, raucous cries blend with the crashing of storms. Being speaks in a demonic voice out of the murky twilight; but the glowing crimson of a winter evening is encircling the world, and a blazing fire directs its light upon the pursuing powers. The flame and smoke of the hearth fire shudder in the holy night before the savage force of the winds.

Blood-glow is Eros and child, is the golden unity of life, and through the eyes of the child, the blood-glow gazes far back into the golden distance (could that be the true significance of the mirror in the Corybantic ring?). In the blood-glow, the mysteries of the maternal universe are revealed. (RR p. 270)

ON THE DEMONIC VISION. Just as messages are transmitted between daemon and soul, so are daemon and soul intimately bound together with the daemonic and primordial source of images, in the living, in a way that transcends the possibility of a purely verbal revelation, for at the moment when the visionary event overwhelms us, we experience, again and yet again, an ever-renewable, cyclical series of "world-beginnings."

We would like to draw the reader's attention to a particularly fiery and colorful strophe composed by Alfred Schuler. It is entitled "Corybantic Dithyramb" (from his "Cosmogony"):

What are you that is more than this my candle-wick,
Than my lamp that boils with its Balsamic oils.
What are you more than my own gentle blossom,
My mosaic of the hyacinths,
Which glow beneath my footfall.
For I am the light that nurtures you.
I am the eye that feigns, at dead of night, a gleam for you.

I am the pearl that shaped its globe within the shell.
I am the rush that youthens our old world,
For I am life...

The world stands in its shining, instantaneous presence there. In the distances of space as well as in the distances of time, everything has, now and forever, its bright light and its sense — even if not so swiftly apprehended within the images. (SW III pp. 426–7)

SCHULER'S SCHOLARSHIP. As an archaeologist, Alfred Schuler, whom I met in 1893, was already in possession of an astonishing wealth of knowledge; he had devised, as it were, a religion of the Magna Mater; he had accumulated, through the most rigorous study of the entire literature of Imperial Rome, a massive amount of material relating to the "chthonic" cults; and he spent all of his time in this enthusiastic frame of mind, whilst he prepared his massive treatise on the swastika for publication (of course, he never finished this work!). Basically, Schuler added nothing that was completely new to the theories devised by Bachofen: but what an astounding fund of material was his! (LK GL p. 1072)

GEORGE AND SCHULER. I have occasionally overheard conversations dealing with the George "Circle"; and I have heard, of course, the story that relates how the name-giver conferred the title "Master" upon himself and the title "young men" upon his acolytes. I have nothing to say regarding the events that transpired in that "circle." But I must insist, in the most decisive terms, that I was the last person in the world to submit to such a "Master." One might even go so far as to say, with equal justice (or injustice!), that Stefan George belonged to the "Klages Circle!" What *can* be demonstrated conclusively (and with accompanying documents) is this: by pure chance, during the decade from 1894–1904, several scientists, artists, and writers congregated in Munich, who sought, by uniting their forces, to present a common front against the Spirit of the age. George was an occasional guest of this group of intellectuals. He seldom became involved in the endless (and often profound) discussions that transpired,

but he was the only person present who could point to the works of his
that had already been published; and he did actually seem eager to provide a focal point to us "new Spirits" when he established his renowned
journal, the *Blaetter für die Kunst*. That is how I became involved with the
man. But let there be no misunderstanding here: if any one person stood
at the very center of things at that time, if there was indeed a master-
spirit in our midst, one who could justly speak of his "following," it was
Alfred Schuler. From him, and from him alone, did I receive the decisive
impetus that determined forever the direction that I would follow in my
metaphysical speculations. (AC p. 381)

THE MYSTICISM OF ALFRED SCHULER. The only true mys-
tic whom I have ever encountered utterly scorned the idea of "making"
anything out of his inspirations. Thus, the notes that Schuler has set down
in the course of his fifty years, which comprise his so-called "aphorisms"
and "fragments," remain, for the most part, almost incomprehensible. *Yet
to the student of symbols these fragmentary remains speak in such an astounding manner as one seldom encounters even in the works of the great
poets!* (LK GL p. 698)

AN AGE UNWORTHY OF ALFRED SCHULER. Bachofen
successfully liberated the image of the primordial soul from the layers of
varnish with which the millennia had covered the remains of prehistory,
so that we were enabled to obtain some inkling as to the inexpressible
beauty of that image. The mission of my own life is to provide the episte-
mological key with which to open up the eyes of man to the profundity
and the truth of Bachofen's discoveries. I was assisted in this mission by the
great good fortune of my encounter with a contemporary thinker, Alfred
Schuler, the student of the ancient "Mysteries," whose investigations were
based in part on the "chthonic" element studied by Bachofen, and in part
on still deeper strata. Schuler was able to walk about like a native on the
landscape of symbolic thought, and the most obvious demonstration of
the authentic nature of his discoveries is surely revealed in the fact that

hardly any of his contemporaries were even aware of the mere fact of their existence! (SW 3 pp. 496–7)

ALFRED SCHULER ON THE BLOOD. Schuler located the spring of every creative power in the blood, which he saw as a glowing substance whose potency could be renewed only by those who were capable of bringing cosmic rebirth to a degenerate age. (LK GL p. 182)

ALFRED SCHULER AND STEFAN GEORGE. Schuler would initiate his lectures with a reading of his most striking fragments; he would begin powerfully, but he would very quickly become seized by an ever-increasing pathos. One might almost say that he began to generate a magnetic field, that he seemed as if transfigured. George would stand behind his chair, becoming increasingly disturbed, until he could no longer conceal his agitation. He finally became extremely pale, and seemed as if he was about to lose his faculties. The psychical atmosphere radiated by Schuler did indeed become overpowering: no one could comprehend precisely whatever it was that took possession of Schuler, but out of that droning voice there suddenly erupted a volcanic flood of glowing lava, and out of the molten stream there arose purple images, unconscious, rapturous.

When the lecture ended, and how it ended, no one could say, but as the visitors began to disperse they were startled to find themselves holding some tattered fragments of a crown that Schuler had torn to pieces in order to bestow them on his guests as he said his farewells.

I then found myself alone with George on the nocturnal streets; he was clutching at my arm, saying: "That's insanity! What have you done, taking me to such a place? It's madness, I tell you! It's unbearable! Take me to a restaurant where the commonplace bourgeois citizen is smoking his cigar and drinking his beer!"

And that's just what I did. (KGL pp. 359–60)

ON STEFAN GEORGE. His soul was essentially *Empire;* this fact accounts for the indirectness of his words, his "impuissance," and his French rigidity; a latter day epigone of the eighteenth century. His character was scheming, destitute, and treacherous: a blend of Catholicism and Renaissance. His character was the coffin that housed his soul. (RR p. 312)

MAGNA MATER. The womanly essence is simply the soul of space, just as the Magna Mater is the soul of the reestablishment of space in the center of time. (SW 2 p. 1350)

MAN, GODS, AND COSMOS. The most profound proposition of all natural law was crystallized in these words of the poet Pindar: "The race of men is one thing, and the race of gods is another; but both receive their life and their breath from the same mother." We broaden the scope of that proposition to state that animals, plants, stars, clouds, and winds are all divine, just as all of the creations that appear within the Cosmos are but leaves upon one stem, and limbs of the same symbiotic formation. (SW 2 p. 1352)

ON RACIAL CONSCIOUSNESS AND COMMUNITY. It is affinity, and not the codification of property law, that moulds the heathen children of the world; the young are formed in the community established by the mother of the tribe, but the adults are formed in the community shaped by the Great Mother of the Cosmos. This affinity manifests itself in the selective breeding that is based upon racial consciousness; it is conquered through actual — or even *symbolical* — mongrelization of the blood. (SW 2 p. 1355)

COSMOS OF MIND, AND COSMOS OF LIFE. The *thought* Cosmos is a mechanical confusion of things; the *living* Cosmos, on the other hand, to which our languages can only allude, cannot be conceptually grasped, for it only reveals itself in the instantaneousness flash of its *here and now* appearance. (SW 2 p. 1367)

"MOTHER RIGHT." Light may still be shed on the phenomenon of the so-called "gynocracy" of prehistory through the application of matriarchal thought to the symbols of water, tree, and moon. Inasmuch as the sensual images of the nocturnal-polar side of the world are at the same time those of the pole-connected "middle," the night must be elevated over the day, the darkness over the light, the below over the above, the fixed over the wandering, space over time, left over right, and so on. Within the human shape, the sensual image of *woman-as-mother* must be elevated over the poles of *man-and-woman*. (SW 2 p. 1374)

LIFE AND SPIRIT. We have bestowed the name *life* upon the all-weaving power of primordial imagery, just as we have given the name *Spirit* to the hostile power that turns those primordial images into hollow phantoms. (SW 2 p. 1239)

TYPES OF CRIMINALITY. There is a potential criminality, which is satisfied merely to peer at naked images of atrocities; and there is even — if one may apply to a strange fact an even stranger name — an *apocryphal* criminality that occurs in those who will not confess their criminal impulses even to themselves. Indeed, whoever closely examines society swiftly discovers the existence of many associations and organizations that provide their clients with a gratuitous satisfaction of criminal impulses. But we must now abandon the soil of true criminality, which always lies in deed and will, and never in the hidden devilry of philosophy, for this question has now taken us beyond our theme, although it is connected with it. It often seems to the psychologist that every halting-station turns out to be a confrontation with the knots in the manifold, interwoven threads of his discourse! (AC p. 222)

THOUGHT AND THE DRIVING FORCES. For the benefit of those students who have not as yet achieved complete familiarity regarding the leading motives of characterological thought, we will here introduce a few remarks that will hopefully enable them to avoid certain misunderstandings.

When we say that the Spirit of a thinker is chiefly determined by a "general current" of human vitality, we are speaking of the inevitable part that his personal system of driving forces plays in this general current; one thing that we must do is to ascertain the degree of the dependence of his thought on his personal driving forces; another, is that we must ascertain the degree of his thought's dependence on the side of his nature that is connected with vitality as such. In brief: the *personal* precondition of thought is not the same as the *vital* precondition of thought. (AC p. 386)

HOSTAGE TO FORTUNE. Doubts and misgivings should certainly be the thinker's priorities; but if a philosopher persists in his doubts, he may place himself in a dangerous position: for a later generation may discover that what it values most in him is his — *backwardness.* (AC p. 3)

SOCRATES THE LOATHSOME. We hear that Socrates was loathsome and impotent, and that he never allowed himself to become intoxicated; we understand thereby how the soil was prepared wherein the faith in the exaggerated worth of the ego could flourish. The rupture must be torn open in the blood before the norms that are hostile to the blood could arise *in the Spirit*...Socrates was a man without contradictions, and, in his eyes, no respect for good breeding could compete with the transcendent value of the rootless individual being. Socrates was a man of the mob, a man without a racial homeland. He was indifferent even to the cycles of the celestial spheres. To Socrates, the torrent, the star, and the cloud were *irrelevant.* (RR p. 425)

PRIMARY AND SECONDARY FEELINGS. We must distinguish between the *primary* feelings, which flow into the act of judgment, and the *secondary,* which spring out of that act. The primary feelings, as is self-evident, comprise any immediate motives, whether they are predominantly internal or whether they arise in the external world. The secondary, on the other hand, are reflexes of already extant feelings. (RR p. 368)

THE ACT OF THE SPIRIT. The spiritual act, flashing out at the stationary point in the swing of the pendulum, seizes the fact within the concept; but flashing out at the instant of the highest animation, the spiritual act seizes, at one and the same moment, object and subject; the bearer of experience and experience itself; the thing, but as habitation of the soul (Idol); and the soul, but as the form of being (Fravashi, "genius," "idea"). Putting the matter somewhat paradoxically, the spiritual act seems to seize the inconceivable, primordial image inasmuch as the image can allow its being conceived. (RR p. 365)

THE POET AND THE IMAGES. The poet is the spiritual form of the ecstatic soul. He breaks through the person to become *image*. Through him speaks the actual character of the Cosmos. The road of degeneration leads from the poet to the metaphysician. The concept is the Caesar of the image, just as logic is the Papacy of the soul. (RR p. 322)

STEFAN GEORGE. We see in Stefan George a poet divided against himself: pagan Eros alongside Christian charity. (LK GL p. 330)

LIFE, AND NOTHING BUT LIFE. Life is everything, and, in reality, what my writings record, and what they will always record, is the tree of life and its golden leaves. (LK GL p. 331)

ON THE DREAMS OF FRIEDRICH HUCH [FROM A LETTER TO HUCH]. Three of your dreams I consider to be more or less "Cosmic" — the one that recounts the far-distant music of the Italian children; the one that deals with the staircase of death; and the one about the vertiginously distant whirling of the solar disc.

Music is a primordial experience, which emerges in manifold guises: but it is always accompanied by nagging, disturbing spectacles. In comparison with all of the ineluctably vanished things, the remainder of life begins to wear a desolate grimace: the pallid face of the specter. One awakens at the beginning to the distant sounds that betoken all of the deepest, most inexpressible experiences of love and beauty; then everything sinks once again into an unfathomable abyss. (LK GL p. 335)

THE CERTAINTIES OF KANT. We must reject as logically untenable Kant's classification of judgments according to their degree of truth, judgments that have been founded in fact upon themselves; although Kant believes that he has comprehended, through the force of his convictions — which he characterizes as "apodictic" certainties — the conditions that validate cognition, he actually has his eye not on the actuality of space, but only on the being of space, space as the object of thought, or our so-called space-object. His incredibly stubborn advocacy of the "a priori" status of perceived space answers the question — or believes, at least, that it has done so — regarding the inviolable nature of the postulates of mathematics, and the Kantian concept of space stands from the outset in the service of Kant's compelling need to provide sufficient grounds to validate the necessary truths of geometry. (SW 1 pp. 142–3)

KANT CONDEMNED OUT OF HIS OWN MOUTH. Jakob Burckhardt has best accounted for that conjunction of greatness and comprehensiveness in Greek spirituality when he noted that without the art of conversation the development of the Greek spirit would have been inconceivable; he said that it was out of the Agora and the Symposium — those favored haunts of Athenian conversationalists — that philosophy itself sprang into being. Regarding this point, we must certainly reject as unjustified (although it is understandable when we consider its source!) Kant's ridicule of ancient Greek thought as a mere "wordy babbling." Without a doubt, a talent for creative thought was originally a function of the talent for lively conversation. (SW 6 p. 659)

CONTRA KANT. We are unable to determine how many other sagacious students share our opinion of Kant, but we can never proceed very far in our reading of the "Critique of Pure Reason" without being astonished that a thinker who devotes himself explicitly to the task of discovering the grounds that make cognition possible should convince himself that he has ascertained those grounds — *in cognition itself!* When Nietzsche, in *Beyond Good and Evil*, says that Kant responds to the question as to how cognition possible by telling us of a "faculty of a faculty," that is only a more drastic expression of the very astonishment that we ourselves experience. (SW 1 p. 141)

KANT AND LEIBNIZ. Kant's investigations give the false impression that he has established the grounds for the possibility of cognition, when what he has really done is to split cognition into two modes, one of which is merely "empirical," while the other allegedly deals with universally valid and necessary truths. This shows us that Kant is merely spinning out the threads of the bungled fabric of Leibnizian thought, which also entails two classes of thought, viz., the class comprising truths of *fact* and that comprising truths of *reason.* (SW 1 p. 142)

THING AND TIME. We have in the thing the inextensible point of connection for the understanding of the temporally fleeting manifold of images; and we have no difficulty in understanding this point as being, as it were, anchored in time. But while the mere temporal site remains where it is, so the thing demands the exact opposite, to be thought of as participating in a span of time, the extreme maximum of which may be as great as the duration of the universe, and the extreme minimum of which may be as brief as the duration of a flash of lightning; but the thing can never be contracted into a tangible point, for there is no "existence" in the mathematical point. (SW 1 p. 23)

TIME AND DURATION. Too few thinkers have devoted their efforts to a successful clarification of the fact that we do not measure the approximate duration of a thing by means of time, but time by means of the duration of a thing. (SW 1 p. 25)

THE BLINDNESS OF FAUST THE CAPITALIST. Without going into the whole question of the visionary symbolism of the second part of *Faust,* we should still draw attention to the disturbing fact that Faust, after a fruitless, storm-tossed life devoted to his own delight, immediately before his death expresses his belief that he experiences his "highest moment" in the consciousness of the praiseworthiness of his labors *as a capitalist entrepreneur* — and here the poet's vision plunges straight into the abyss — but Faust is too arrogant to hear, at that very moment, the sound of the spade that is digging his own grave! (SW 1 p. 65)

EXISTENCE AND PREDICATES. The thing is the original "entity" and the immediate paradigm and exemplar of the substantive in general; hence, the history of human thought provides countless instances which illustrate the misleading thing-status of such concepts as: process, fate, life, childhood, age, youth, morning, evening, spring, enmity, sin, and so on *ad infinitum.* Precisely herein lies the basis of the fact that in so many languages the utilization of the word "exists" [*Sein*] signifies the mere connection of the predicate-word with the affirmative statement. Every judgment regarding time as well as every judgment regarding space is so constructed as to mislead us into the belief that there actually *is* a "time-thing," and that there really *exists* a "space-thing!" (SW 1 pp. 24–5)

SOUL AND SPIRIT. The character of the soul is sometimes impulsive, and at other times it may be enthusiastically abandoned; so by contrast the character of Spirit appears in the light of an obstruction that realizes its potential in the intentional binding of a psychical emotion! Accordingly, an equilibrium between soul and Spirit can never be reached; and what may seem to us to be an example of an achieved and gracious balance between soul and Spirit in an outstanding personality, e.g., the poise of a Goethe, can be shown, under more rigorous scrutiny, to be merely a matter of compromise, an instance of artistic "style." As such, this state can never be attained without a patent loss in psychical immediacy. (SW 1 p. 74)

CONNECTIONS. The error of the "Panlogicians," if we might just borrow their favorite expression for a moment, stems from the "equivocation" that confuses connection in general with a perceived connection. The Panlogicians have correctly stated the fact that only the spiritual act can establish connections; but they have overlooked the fact that there are two species of connections which can be established through comprehension: the conceptual connection of one point to another point; and the non-conceptual connection of point to happening. (SW 1 p. 85)

THIS IS OUR TRUTH. There is a being from outside the world of space and time, called "Spirit" (*logos, nous*), which is capable of driving every critical nature into one and the same conceptual scheme, i.e., one that is based on unity, quantification, and measurement, and that forces critical individuals to observe the temporal actuality under the guise of a system of interconnected quantifiable points. An excessive emphasis upon factuality and upon the universally binding force of truth is from the outset the expression of the monotonous quality of the faculty of judgment in every nature who yields to this impulse and who possesses this capacity. (SW 1 p. 62)

TRUTH AND DISCOVERY. All truths are equally valuable — or equally valueless — if we value them merely because they are true. In other words, we possess no general yardstick that can accurately evaluate a truth, so long as we focus exclusively upon the finished *product* instead of upon the *process* whereby that truth came into existence. (SW 1 p. 122)

DIFFERENT MODES OF THOUGHT ENTIRELY. Such thinkers as Giordano Bruno and Carl Gustav Carus seldom augment the fund of knowledge that was acquired by such scholars as Isaac Newton and Charles Darwin. Conversely, rarely do we find the second pair adding to the knowledge of the first. (SW 1 p. 127)

SEEKERS AFTER TRUTH. The alleged lack of bias in those who "search for truth" is a pious deception concocted by a superficial mentality that is overawed by the mere *title* of "science." (SW 1 p. 130)

THE INDIVISIBLE UNION. We take this opportunity to explain why we arrange colors and seeing, sounds and hearing, and smells and smelling in polar contrast to each other. Everyone recognizes that we can never achieve a satisfactory philosophical demonstration when we are required to associate the following expressions: invisible colors, inaudible sounds, and "unsmellable" smells; it is thereby conceded that not only can there be no seeing without colors, no hearing without sounds, and no smelling without smells; but there are also no colors without visibility, no sounds without audibility, and no smells without a capacity to smell them. The appearance and the faculty that enables one to experience it thus occur in an indivisible union. (SW 1 p. 103)

PHILOSOPHICAL ARROGANCE. Ever since the discovery of the Platonic "Doctrine of the Ideas," there has obviously never been a definitive settlement of the controversy between those who hold that the "universals" exist only in the thinking consciousness and those who maintain that they constitute the driving and formative powers of actuality itself. Modern thinkers have only picked up where the medieval scholastics left off. Today's philosophers, who pride themselves on having solved the great riddle that split all the best philosophical heads in medieval Europe into the two great camps of "realists" and "nominalists," *are only fooling themselves.* (SW 1 p. 109)

MAN AND WOMAN. We avert our gaze from the "emancipation" movement of modern times, to see that woman, throughout all of recorded history, is the bearer of the powers of life and soul, just as man is always the bearer of the powers of Spirit and productive activity; this holds true even today for the vast majority of men and women. (SW 6 p. 664)

TEARS AND CRYING. It astonishes us that Darwin, whose chapter on weeping [in *The Expression of the Emotions*] provides the richest material to establish a conclusive demonstration of the detachability of the act of *shedding tears* from the act of *crying,* could not free himself, on speculative grounds, from a need to maintain the inseparability of the two phenomena. (SW 6 p. 667)

VITAL AND MECHANICAL MOVEMENTS. Darwin, along with his predecessors and his disciples, basically recognizes only one species of movement, the *mechanical,* and he is involuntarily led by a compulsion to cancel out the *vital* movement and to put mechanical movement in its place. (SW 6 p. 199)

EXPRESSIVE MOVEMENT. To every inner activity belongs its analogous movement; or, if one uses "movement" instead of activity: *every inner movement entails its analogous outer movement.* (SW 6 p. 681)

PHYSIOGNOMICAL INTERPRETATION. Lavater already understood the principle whereby we can evaluate mimicry *physiognomically.* Thus, whoever possesses the quality of an energetic will, often finds himself in a condition of nervous tension; he who is by nature fearful, will find himself, again and again, in a condition of anxiety; and the habitually short-tempered man will more often than not find himself in a condition of anger. (SW 6 p. 679)

EXPRESSIVE MOVEMENTS. To every inner condition there corresponds, as its expression, those bodily movements that portray that condition. (SW 6 p. 678)

THE SCIENCE OF FACT AND THE SCIENCE OF APPEARANCE. General logic, as it is understood today, reveals itself as a skeletal structure, within which an almost endless series of philosophical procedures find a place, and in which every logical proposition find its application. That which had been inaugurated as a mere "methodology," is now the most informative jumping-off point for differentiating between the intellectual technique employed by the practical man and that employed by the theoretical, the technique of the manual worker from that employed by the scholar, the musician's technique from the mathematician's, and so on. However, in our own field of research, that which we hold to be securely established...is the sharp distinction that must be drawn between two species of thought: the predominantly *conceptual* and the predominantly *allusive* modes, or the study of *fact* and the study of *appearance*. (SW 6 p. 656)

PSYCHOLOGY AND METAPHYSICS. Some students renounce even the possibility of a significant conceptualization of the soul, and they assure us that we have immediate access only to the "phenomena of consciousness"; others refer to psychology as the science of "inner" (immediate) experience, from which viewpoint it is not any very great distance to today's repeated revivals of the doctrine of "inner perception"; others remain encamped in the antiquated "Doctrine of the Soul [*Seelenlehre*]," notwithstanding the fact that they cannot provide a satisfactory explanation of the unique nature of that soul. And, once again, there are still others for whom psychology appears to constitute merely one branch of the neurology; and again, others, who, scenting in every one of these doctrines a false "naturalism," promise to bestow upon us a novel and refined species of thought, sometimes of the "intuitive" variety, and at others of the "subjective" type, which we are told will enable us to avoid every stumbling-block that is placed on our path by erroneous preconceptions. All honor to the rigor of our investigators! But we think that here a great expense will be unprofitable due to their mindless hostility to the perpetually unavoidable *metaphysics*. Whichever of the renowned — or obscure — conceptual determinations that one adopts, one will find oneself in the midst of metaphysics, and one will become so much more seriously entangled in self-contradictory basic assumptions, the more one feels obliged to repudiate metaphysics.

Consider: The discussion of the "phenomena of consciousness" leads one directly to the question regarding the nature of consciousness, and then to the nature of the unconscious, and, before one realizes it, one is confronted with questions regarding monism, dualism, or even "psychophysical parallelism"...But the believer in the soul, on the other hand, is already graced by the seal of "ontology," and he already manifests as well the clearest antithesis to the materialism of the neurologists.

The odd thing about the speculations of our "intuitionists" and "subjectivists" is the fact that both types remain united in their habitual, albeit unconscious, *Platonism*...

No one has the right to discuss psychology unless and until he has become a *metaphysician.* (SW 1 pp. 5–6)

THE RAGE OF HERACLES. The Spirit, once it had liberated itself from servitude to life, proceeded autocratically, becoming the unchained force of destruction; the activity of thought becomes hereafter the tool of the will to power. During this perhaps Heraclitean phase, life becomes dependent upon Spirit, thought becomes dependent upon will, and the main purpose of mankind, without as well as within, is to enslave "nature," so that man may celebrate the triumph of Spirit in the "miracles of technology." Thus, we realize that it was no accident when the first disciples of the rule of an alleged "world-principle," the Stoics, chose Heracles as their exemplary hero. (SW 1 p. 753)

SCHOLAR AND PHILOSOPHER. The scholar feels the greatest affection for that which is *certain;* the philosopher, on the other hand, loves the *hypothetical* above all else. (SW 4 p. 26)

ABSTRACTION AND EXPRESSION. So-called abstract thought is the most introspective manifestation of affective life, i.e., it is the least likely to be converted into visible bodily movements. (SW 4 p. 26)

BURCKHARDT AS CHARACTEROLOGIST. Now and forever, Jakob Burckhardt's greatest service was in applying—perhaps unintentionally — the *characterological* approach to the cultural historiography of diverse ages and nations. Therefore, for every characterologist, Burckhardt's *History of Greek Civilization, The Culture of the Renaissance in Italy,* and *The Age of Constantine the Great,* are required reading. (SW 4 p. 479)

EAST AND WEST. The extra-spatio-temporal power to which we have applied the name "Spirit" strives to kill the unity of life by severing the poles that bind body to soul; by binding itself to the body-pole in order to exorcise the soul, Spirit deprives the body of that soul. Here, however, a question arises: might not Spirit form an alliance with the soul, in order to cause the body to wither, thus disembodying the soul? Might it not be upon that path that we must locate the interpretation of actuality that ascribes different degrees of being to the character of (deceptive) appearances? With the affirmative answer we have probed the deepest reasons for the opposition of every species of Platonism to Chinese Taoism, and, what's more, we have reached the very point at which the Asian style of approach to actuality diverges most sharply from that of the West. (SW 1 p. 339)

SOUL AND MASK. The entity that places so many obstacles before us as we attempt to devise a science of the soul is not — the *soul,* but the *masquerade* of the soul, which the will to power thrusts between the soul and the observer. Thus, the student who insists upon penetrating every mask in order to approach the soul's true visage, has already proceeded far along the path to an authentic comprehension of characterology. (PEN p. 62)

WHAT IS LIFE? Although the natural scientific theory of life ("Biology") places the problem of life in the forefront, science has certainly not been able to solve it. Biologists occupy themselves with two groups of entities, i.e., the living and the non-living, but they have come up with no answer as to whence the "living-ness" of the living entity originates. There are no sensual qualities through which the living may be conclusively distinguished from the non-living. All colors, sounds, tastes, scents, textures, formal configurations, and types of movement, can be found in both spheres. The first substantial solution to this problem was hit upon, centuries before the common era, by the Pythagorean physician Alcmaeon, who held that only the living being possesses the capacity to "move itself." But even here, although we will concede that self-motility may well be an *expressive indication* of life, it is certainly not a *characteristic quality* of living things. (SW 3 pp. 250–1)

THINGS IN SPACE AND TIME. Every thing, in every moment, has its place in *space;* and a thing may "exist" for a shorter, or a longer, duration in *time.* Every quality of a thing, since it participates in that thing (even when that quality is merely "mediated"), has, in turn, its necessary connection to space and time. Thus, whether it is a thing, or a quality, or a process, every conceivable "it-point" must be distinguished from the vitality of the *happening* in that it has that very character of a point; in addition, it has the character of a *point-of-connection.* (SW 1 p. 84)

THE TYPE AND THE INSTANCE. When we scrutinize the lives of the various individuals to whom Nietzsche applied the name "master-type" — in addition to [Mirabeau and Napoleon], mention must be made of Julius Caesar, Friedrich II Hohenstaufen, Cesare Borgia, and Frederick the Great — we can scarcely avoid the impression that this "master-type" is merely an ingenious and poetic day-dream, to which none of the aforesaid individuals bore even the remotest resemblance. (PEN p. 126)

THE ULTIMATE THULE. The life of Nietzsche's soul, in comparison with that of our Classical and Romantic writers, because of its unrealistic needs and the glittering filigree of its thought, stands at the border: one step beyond, and we are in a world of the hollow ornament, the side-show, the *mask.* (AC p. 375)

NIETZSCHE AND "THE MAN OF FEELINGS." There can be no greater error than to confuse Nietzsche's restless vibrancy with the temperamental ebullition of the "man of feelings," to whom Nietzsche is the most extreme contrast that the mind can conceive. As one who is in his inmost core asocial, who stands wholly within his own…vital nature, the "affairs of the heart" only interest Nietzsche to the extent that he is their *critic and judge.* (AC p. 374)

THE ELEMENTAL VISION. I marvel at the greatness of Nietzsche's humanity…Nevertheless, regarding greatness as well as smallness, strength as well as weakness: life never reveals its secrets in such things… What Nietzsche has to say about such matters is great, viewed from the standpoint of humanity, but his words are certainly not a revelation of life. What I have always sought in life — and what I have also found — leads me to the following reflection: if only there still lived within my soul that primordial homeland of which I received such a spectacular vision in vanished years; if only there were still men upon the earth who possessed the power that could renew the mysteries of the cosmic night; if only there still were eyes that could penetrate to the ocean floor above which pulsates the surging of metallic billows. Such things as these are life to me. Such things allow me to plunge myself into the hot glow of the elemental forces. (RR p. 522)

ON NIETZSCHE'S VIEW OF THE PRIESTLY CASTE. Nietzsche sees the Jews as the race that has devised the most powerful and influential priestly caste in history…We will now provide a tentative explanation that might account for what seem to be peculiar discrepancies in his estimation of the Jews. He directs his gaze upon the depth, strength, endurance, absolutism, and relentlessness of the priestly will to power; upon its incomparable sagacity, cunning, and craftiness in the selection of mediators; and upon its ingenious flair for adaptation and re-interpretation: thus, he admires the priest and, consequently, the Jew, as the consummate manifestations of the priestly caste. On the other hand, he faces the fact that the priestly will, which is based upon life-envy, is directed against life; this will infects life, poisons life, and causes life to degenerate: thus, Nietzsche becomes the passionate enemy of the priest and, again, of the Jew, as the most extreme embodiments of diseased life. We consider the admiration and the opposition to be two inseparably linked sides of one and the same fact, and we therefore conclude that neither the priestly embodiment nor the Jewish embodiment constitute a comprehensive representation of that which they both serve. Therefore, just as Nietzsche borrowed the name of a renowned god for his cult of Dionysus, so are we justified in borrowing the name of a hostile counterpart in speaking of the cult of Yahweh. There is no disputing the fact that Nietzsche was inflexible in his conviction that historical Christianity is the religion of St. Paul. *And the religion of St. Paul is merely a particular version of the cult of Yahweh.* (PEN pp. 152–3)

WHAT GERMAN LITERATURE LACKS.

There is no German prose as yet…We still do not possess a creative writer whose deep feeling for the German language has enabled him to escape this dilemma. Goethe is "Rococo" — Jean Paul is downright *old-fashioned* — Hölderlin has the strongest rhythmic sense of the three, but he devoted himself primarily to poetry — and Stefan George is scarcely to be mentioned in this connection. Of all our great writers, only Nietzsche had sufficient talent to repair the omission, but even he spoiled his greatest achievement, the *Zarathustra*, by adulterating his own style (alas!) with the Germanic idioms of Luther's Bible. In brief: *we still await the creator of a German prose.* (LK GL p. 341)

FALSE AND TRUE IN NIETZSCHE.

The best, the deepest, and the truest of all the discoveries that Nietzsche has won for the philosophy of life comprise the fragments of a philosophy of "orgiastics." *Everything else is worthless.* We must see this clearly, so that we can comprehend the motives behind his critique of the substrate-concept as well as the ultimate significance of his Heracliteanism. We must also perceive, through the breach that he opened up in the meters-thick cocoon that shielded delusion's chimera, the road to new truths, and even to a whole new species of thought. However, Nietzsche himself could not set out upon that road, so that we must content ourselves by widening the breach that he opened. (PEN p. 168)

FORMULA. Every one of Nietzsche's truths derives from the *pagan* side of his character; all of his errors reflect his *Christian* side. (PEN p. 180)

DIONYSUS AGAINST THE SPIRIT. Nietzsche does not see the "Dionysian" predominantly as the alleged counterpart to the "Apollonian"; rather, his viewpoint springs from a profound opposition to everything that is *spiritual* — and most of all to *the disaster of consciousness.* (PEN p. 166)

NIETZSCHE'S MARKSMANSHIP. Nietzsche's judicial investigations into the phenomenon of "life-envy" hit the bull's-eye time and time again, and his discoveries in this area would retain their fundamental significance even if his "master-type" should turn out in the end to be only a thrilling phantom. (PEN p. 127)

FRIEDRICH NIETZSCHE: THE WORLD'S "FIRST PSYCHOLOGIST." There are two reasons why we must call Nietzsche the "first psychologist." The first is that he took upon himself, as his major mission, the task of illuminating the historical evolution of *general* value judgments; this enabled him to construct a propaedeutic for every possible science of the soul. The second was his utilization of this method to scrutinize *particular* value judgments in order to determine whether or not they constituted critical instantiations of the "will to power"; in such cases, Nietzsche could conclusively demonstrate the presence of *self-deception.* (PEN p. 65)

NIETZSCHE, PARMENIDES, AND "SOCRATISM." Nietzsche stated (in the volume of his literary remains entitled "The Will to Power"):

"Parmenides said: 'one cannot think what is not'; we take hold of the other end of the stick, and say: *what cannot be thought, must be a fiction.*" The remark is as profound as it is true, if, in fact, it is an expression of the utter inimitability of the condition of judgment and that of actuality; it may be deeply misleading, however, if the word "fiction" is being used here to demonstrate the impossibility of our ever ascertaining the truth. In fact, Nietzsche remained throughout his life bogged down in *Socratism,* which accounts for the fact that he never pressed through to a clearer distinction between truth and actuality. (SW 1 p. 118)

ON NIETZSCHE'S HANDWRITING. We have encountered no handwritten exemplar from the entire period extending from German Classicism to the turn of the twentieth century that bears the slightest resemblance to that of Nietzsche…There is something uniquely radiant, bright, shining like silk, something, as it were, ethereal; it manifests an obvious lack of warmth; this is a man who, although he is deeply rooted in the home, must rise to ever higher, ever colder heights (like the albatross in his poem of that name), one who has only the slightest connection with the profound subterranean depths, for he sees the world solely through the wide-ranging gaze of the Spirit. It is precisely in the *downwards* and the *below* that he can see only the "abyss." There is something in this script that is transparent, crystalline — the complete antithesis to the cloudy, the miasmal, the elastic, the gushing, the surging; there is something uncannily hard, sharp, of a glass-like fragility, with a complete absence of the conciliatory — something utterly formed, complete, even, one might say, chiseled…Never before have we encountered an unstylized handwriting that manifested such sharpness and angularity, together with an utterly flawless distribution of the handwritten masses and a sequential organization that almost reminds one of a string of precious pearls! (AC pp. 344–375)

NIETZSCHE AS SOCRATIC THINKER. When we examine certain aspects of Nietzsche's theory of judgment-formation — especially with regard to his opposition to the very notion of the "substrate-concept" — we feel that the customary imputation of a passionate anti-Socratism to Nietzsche is well deserved. His own explicit diatribes in *The Birth of Tragedy* and *The Genealogy of Morals* seem to leave no room for doubt in this regard. Thus, how astonished we are when we encounter other aspects of his thought: for then we see Nietzsche falling into Socratism himself, and even into a rootless skepticism, which he embodies in concepts that he often wields as the lethal weapons with which he seeks to destroy *his own discoveries* — even when this very procedure is plunging his entire philosophical enterprise into an all-embracing chaos of logical inconsistencies! (PEN p. 181)

A NEGATIVE ASPECT OF NIETZSCHE'S PSYCHOLOGY.

The human spirit — not the living organism — is conversant with anarchy: thus, this thinker who had hitherto served as the greatest breaker of chains in the history of mankind, in the end must logically join forces with all of the revolutionaries who went before. Thus, it is not the body — this eternal *here and now,* this sad and joyous event — that possesses the capacity to wish; on the contrary, it is Spirit, restlessly oscillating between *time past* and *time to come,* which participates in vitality, but this occurs solely through the mediation of the wish. So we find that Nietzsche consistently howls his rage against the man of the wish and his vampiric "ideals"; he brings to light, as none of his predecessors had ever succeeded in doing, the paradoxical analogy that subsists between the madness of purposefulness and the mummification of the past. The protest of life against the arrogance of consciousness he locates in the protest of the body against the "holy Spirit" *within!*...Nietzsche's works were born out of the innermost needs of his being and out of his, as it were, *self-flagellation.* Without a doubt, his productions are vulnerable to the grave accusation that they are redolent of personal biases that render them both dangerous and deceiving. (PEN p. 82)

THE WISDOM OF LORD BYRON. Under the legend "Sorrow is Knowledge" [*Gram ist Erkenntnis*], Nietzsche cites the following verse of Lord Byron's:

> *Sorrow is knowledge: those who know the most*
> *Must mourn the deepest o'er the fatal truth,*
> *The Tree of Knowledge is not that of life.*

Now although these lines could hardly have been intended by their author for the purposes to which we will put them, the factual content of Byron's words entitles us to propose them as the master thesis of a pagan method of cognition, for they point an admonishing finger at the relationship of life to consciousness, and of experience to knowledge, and they perform this office from a perspective that recognizes the genuine processes that pose a threat to life. (PEN pp. 189–90)

NIETZSCHE: PHILO-SEMITE AND GERMANOPHOBE

I. Nietzsche had so little of the "anti-Semite" in his nature that he can scarcely conceive of a more loathsome character than the: "anti-Semite!" Whoever takes the pains to examine Nietzsche's collected works in order to determine his actual opinion of the Jews — and of the *Germans* — cannot fail to arrive at the following conclusions: Nietzsche held the Jews in the highest possible esteem; he detests all "anti-Semites"; and he hated the Germans with a blind hatred...

Had Nietzsche lived into the era of the "World War," there can be no doubt as to whom he would have pledged his allegiance: he would certainly have sided with the mortal enemies of Germany! (PEN p. 152)

EROS AND DAEMON. Nietzsche's world is a world of egos, of characters, or, if you prefer, of great personalities; his is a Renaissance world. Nietzsche wished for great, profound, truthful men (his "superman" is no longer merely a man!). Only rarely does he break out of this circle. In general, however, it remains a world of persons, a world whose depths harbor yearning always, but fulfillment *never*...Nietzsche understood neither Eros nor the demonic. We, on the other hand, can understand the one or the other; but only an omniscient thinker can understand them both. (RR p. 522)

NIETZSCHE: PHILO-SEMITE AND GERMANOPHOBE II.

It is Nietzsche who informs us that the Jews who have bestowed the "most refined manners" upon Europe.

It is Nietzsche who informs us that the Jews are the great masters of the art of adaptation, the true geniuses of European drama.

It is Nietzsche who praises the Jews as the race that has the most reverence for their forefathers.

It is Nietzsche who finds in the "Old Testament" the best criteria for distinguishing the "great" from the "small."

It is Nietzsche who holds that "In comparison with Luther's Bible, all other books are mere 'literature.'"

It is Nietzsche who insists that the Jews and the Romans are the two most spiritually virile nations in history.

It is Nietzsche who tells us that the Jews initiated the "grand style" in moral matters...

It is Nietzsche who informs us that the Jews are "the most ancient and best-bred of all the races."

It is Nietzsche who urges the "noble officers of Prussia" to marry Jewesses in order to create "a new ruling caste for Europe."

It is Nietzsche who calls the Bible "the most profound and most important" book in existence.

It is Nietzsche who tells us that the Jews have raised "the dream of ethical nobility to a higher plane than has any other people."

It is Nietzsche who tells us that the ideas of the Jews are the means by which Europe has achieved its masterful position.

It is Nietzsche whose exaggerated regard for the writings of Heine betrays him into such statements as the following: "Heine's style is far superior to anything that mere Germans" (!) can hope to achieve!

And similar reflections can be culled *by the dozen* from Nietzsche's works! (PEN pp. 223–4)

OASIS OF THE SOUL. Even in the midst of the nineteenth century, with its technology and its worship of hard facts, we must acclaim, as an oasis in the growing wasteland of "progress," the dream-laden *philosophy of life* of the German Romantics and the militant *religion of life* of Friedrich Nietzsche! (SW 3 p. 364)

NIETZSCHE UNBOUND AND NIETZSCHE IN CHAINS. It can be demonstrated that Nietzsche — this greatest breaker of chains in the history of mankind — was himself a man in chains. While he advances the perfection to be achieved in the extra-personal fullness of ecstatic moments on one side, on the other he discovers — the "superman" and his restless ascent to ever more wretched heights! What Nietzsche himself annihilates from the ground up: *the enslavement of life to purposes and to the future,* he restores on another plane, so that he finally appears to be intent upon annihilating *himself* in a veritable frenzy of "self-overcomings." (SW 4 p. 707)

NIETZSCHE IN A NUTSHELL. The following is without a doubt the most elegant formula whereby we can express Nietzsche's true nature: he was the battlefield between the orgiastic celebrants, whom he was the first to identify and interpret, and the ascetic priestly caste, which he was, here again, the first to unmask for us...To employ the language of myth, Nietzsche was simply the field of battle whereon Dionysus and Yahweh waged their war. We know of no comparable example in all of world history. We have often encountered, and still do encounter, the antithesis: Dionysus vs. Socrates, or, more commonly, Dionysus vs. Yahweh. But that one and the same personality should be possessed by both Dionysus and Yahweh is the most terrible case that the mind can conceive. (PEN p. 210)

THE NIETZSCHEAN ERUPTION. The author of these lines can well remember — as can the majority of his colleagues who came to maturity during those heady days of the 1890s, and with whom he has often discussed this matter — the explosive impact exerted upon all of us when we first succumbed to the sorcery of Nietzsche's thought. The effect can only be compared to a raging typhoon, a massive earthquake, or a volcanic eruption…

At the very instant when we begin to read Nietzsche's books, we feel as if we had been dragged into a magic coach that hurtles at dizzying velocity through infinite landscapes. We are plunged into the bowels of the earth, then we are dropped onto icy glaciers and mountain summits, and all the while the world is shining with a harsh and intense radiance, which is sometimes terrible and threatening, but which is always violent and overpowering. (PEN p. 11)

THE LAST, DYING WAVE OF ROMANTICISM. The Romantics constituted the ultimate wave, because the very core of terrestrial life died when they died. Surely man has never experienced, nor has he ever suffered more rapturously, the convulsions of being than did the Romantics. Their horizon flamed in the fiery gloaming of farewell, a last, irrevocable severing of the ties.

Only a select few perceived this event. Fewer still understood its implications. Even Nietzsche confused that melancholy and overpowering radiance with the first flush of a new dawn.

I have indulged in such descriptions merely so that the reader might be able to see the reason why we refer to these last, great bearers of the radiance of earth as the dithyrambic bards of destruction. They were surrounded by ghouls and vampires, and their creative work was never really consummated.

The whole earth reeks as never before with the blood of the slaughtered, and the apelike masses now strut about with the precious spoils that they have plundered from the ravaged temple of life! (SW II p. 923)

BIOLOGY AND HEURISTIC EXPEDIENCY. Naturalists, as well as philosophers, repeatedly emphasize the fact that it is impossible to draw a hard and fast line between the animal realm and the plant realm, since there exists no unexceptionable criterion of distinction between the

two. Those who would ponder the biological borderlands must content themselves by examining the preponderant "weight of the evidence" on a case-by-case basis. (SW 2 pp. 1081–2)

DUALITY AND POLARITY. The duality of subject and object rests upon the polarity of *experiencing* life and *appearing* event. (SW 3 p. 49)

FORMS OF POLARITY. A relationship of polarity exists between positive and negative magnetism, between right hand and left, and between male and female in sexually dimorphous species. (SW 3 pp. 52–3)

G. F. DAUMER I. G. F. Daumer never employed the term "Spirit" in our comprehensive and technical sense, for he restricted his meditations to the Spirit of Christianity and to such "Catholic" converts as "Protestantism" and the "secret societies." Nevertheless, in spite of the fact that Daumer was certainly not what we would call a *psychologist,* we have no hesitation in seeing him as a profound *culture-critic* and as the indisputable forerunner of Nietzsche's "Antichrist." (SW 2 p. 902)

G. F. DAUMER II. The Romantic writer Daumer published in 1847 a work entitled *The Mysteries of Christian Antiquity*; in this volume, Daumer, basing his theories in part upon records and traditions, and in part upon familiar symbols and customs, demonstrates conclusively that ancient Christianity was, in reality, a sect devoted to the appalling god Moloch, whose worshippers have maintained, through uninterrupted millennia, the practice of cultic cannibalism [*kultischer Anthropophagie*]. Daumer enriches his speculations by adducing profound observations of Bayle (whose meditations are still worthy of perusal even today), which might provide, all things considered, a literal basis for Nietzsche's accusation: "Christianity is the metaphysics of the hangman." Daumer's book provides the student of the secret history of Christianity with the most dazzling wealth of material that we have ever encountered. (PEN p. 154)

SPIRIT, THE DESTROYER. As Spirit penetrates deeper and deeper into the life-cell, it transforms both body and soul. The changes are expressed in the physiognomy of the body as well as in the ascent of technology. In the arena of the soul the effects of Spirit lead immediately to alterations in the emotional life, which find expression in the dwindling of poetic and artistic creativity. In the end, Spirit can only express itself through the medium of "ideas." (SW 2 913)

SPIRIT AND HISTORY. Historical man is the battleground whereon two forces struggle for supremacy: actuality, which we call *life,* and an acosmic power, which we call *Spirit.* (SW 2 p. 912)

EXPERIENCE AND JUDGMENT. The pole of experience corresponds to the pole of the *phenomenal* world; the pole of judgment corresponds to the pole of the *objective* world. AG p. 74)

VOLITION AND EXPRESSION. The direction of volition is determined by the *individual,* but the expressive movement is determined by the *species.* (AG p. 72)

EXPRESSION AND SYMBOL. The expressive movement is to the volitional movement as the living symbol is to the factual judgment: in brief, *the expressive movement is the symbol of the action.* (AG p. 72)

ON SPACE. Perceived space is essentially different from mathematical space. Mathematical space is infinite; perceived space is finite. In mathematical space, the dimensions are interchangeable; this is not the case with perceived space. Thus, in perceived space, we find an actual *over* and an actual *under;* an actual *before* and an actual *behind;* and an actual *left* and an actual *right.* Mathematical space is colorless and silent; perceived space is filled with color and sound. Mathematical space is disembodied; perceived space is embodied. (AG pp. 117–8)

WHAT IS "GRAPHOLOGY?" The word "Graphology" certainly does not mean: "the science of writing." Its real meaning is the doctrine that treats handwriting as one of the expressions of character; it comprises as well the scientific investigation of the ultimate origins of the writing movement. These are, obviously, rooted in the bodily constitution. Movements sometimes possess a psychical content; sometimes they are devoid of such content. Most of the so-called "reflex processes" — coughing, sneezing, blinking of the eyes, increased production of saliva while eating, the flexing of the skeletal structure while reaching down to touch the floor, and even in the trembling movement that we find so often in the elderly — are without psychical content. On the other hand, other actions — such as the grasping of a book, which no one doubts originates in the conscious fact of an act of will — do possess a psychical content. Now there exists no fact of consciousness "in- and for-itself," but only as a condition of a living personality. Thus, in every volitional movement personality plays the key role. (SW 8 p. 703)

HISTORY OF GRAPHOLOGY. Graphology has a "prehistory" as well as a history in the strict sense. The prehistory reaches as far back as the Renaissance. We can name dozens of students who shared the conviction that there was a characterological value in the analysis of handwriting. We point to Hocquart in France and Henze in Germany (Henze would later be active in Sweden) as noteworthy exponents of early graphology. This pre-history came to an end when the French researcher Michon published his renowned *System of Graphology* in 1875. In that treatise, the author — who was a profound student of man — set down the observations that he had made over a thirty-year period. He believed that he had discovered revealing correspondences between character-traits and handwritten exemplars.

The history of Graphology in the proper sense belongs exclusively to the German lands, and this development can best be examined in the three following works, all of which embody decisive advances over the previous efforts: Wilhelm Preyer's *On the Psychology of Writing* (first issued in 1895;

second edition brought out by Leopold Voss of Leipzig); Georg Meyer's *The Scientific Foundations of Graphology* (first edition in 1901; subsequent editions published by Fischer of Jena); and, finally, my own *Handwriting and Character* (which made its first appearance in 1901; later editions were published by J. A. Barth of Leipzig). (SW 8 p. 803)

WHITE NIGHT. This night is harshly bright, like coldly ringing glass. An imperceptible flood seems to have seized everything that lives in its embrace, and even dead things stare, as with sallow gaze, into a dangerous domain. Massive dark-green cloud-waves roll throughout the heavens. Whitish breakers shine brightly above hidden reefs. Moonlight drips through the cracks and crevices. Signals swiftly sound and flash in the deep blue of the distance. A paler haze rises high above the towers of the great city. (RR p. 232)

ON THE GREATNESS OF E. M. ARNDT. Thanks to Arndt's renowned and passionate love of the German fatherland — in the noblest sense of that expression — he became the deadliest critic of the very century in which he had been born — i.e., the 18th. He established the fact that all of the defects, blunders, and weaknesses of that age had their source in its "rationalism," i.e., its cult of reason, in which Arndt saw the workings of Spirit, which separates itself from the soul, from the body, and, ultimately, "from the earth." Thenceforth, he scrutinized the entire history of western man from the same thematic perspective; he concluded that every defect, blunder, and weakness to be found in Europe's entire past derives from the destructive workings of the identical divisive force: Spirit. (SW 2 p. 902)

THOUGHT AND SYMBOL. One may well ask if there exists a fundamentally different species of cognition [from the logical sort], which, so to speak, utilizes its own concepts so as to enable us to hold fast to our living experience. There is indeed such a species of cognition, and we find it in the *symbolic thought* of prehistoric cultures. (SW 3 p. 332)

ON MODERN THOUGHT. Today we are witnessing an unprecedented "de-naturing" of thought, and we should not deceive ourselves: it will ultimately end in the complete ignorance of a new dark age. (SW 3 p. 333)

THE DECLINE OF THOUGHT. For about a century now the foreground of research into the human sciences has been occupied by psychology — literally, "the science of the soul" — which, in its turn, presupposes the existence of "biology" (literally, "the science of life"), since the concept of the soul can have no meaning in the absence of a living essence in which it may dwell. But when we look back at the achievements of the so-called "Romantic Philosophy," we must acknowledge that ever since the Romantic period, we have managed to entangle ourselves in all sorts of confusion in our utilization of basic concepts, so that philosophy now threatens to yield completely to systematic doubt ("skepticism"); it seems that we are about to renounce the very idea of knowledge itself! While man's adherence to the example of the mechanistic "world-view" has allowed him to pile up mountains of "facts," and while the engineering of his dazzling apparatus has enabled him to achieve the greatest precision in experimental research, he has long since forgotten just why he has need of all this extravagance! (SW 3 p. 332)

ON VEILS AND MYSTERIES. Mysteries...neither desire to be, nor *can* they be, "unriddled." A mystery from which the veil that obscures it has been torn is, indeed, no longer a mystery at all. Those who respect the integrity of the concealing veil are those natures who prefer metaphysics to any form of "redemption." The actualization of a primordial mystery transforms it into "cognition." One should never inquire into the primal origins; but one can ask all sorts of questions about essences, such as the essence of light, the essence of science, or even, if you wish, the essence of the copula "and!" (SW 3 pp. 332–3)

CONCEPT AND MEANING. The concept, as it were, *belongs* to the meaning of the word. The concept is related to the meaning — if we might employ an analogy — as the minute crystal is related to the matrix-solution from which it has been precipitated at the moment when the crystal separates from the solution and its form is rigidly fixed. The concept can be defined, but the meaning-content of a word *never*. The concept thinks through the medium of the word; the meaning-content can only be experienced on the basis of a profound feeling for language. The concept can be permanently established; but the meaning-content only mocks those who would place it in shackles. (AG pp. 212–3)

ON THE "ACTUALITY OF THE IMAGES." All primitive cultures have experienced that which the critical rigor of the Greeks also brought to consciousness: *the enhancement of the actual.* Since we tend to confuse actuality with being, it appears to us as nonsensical when we witness the whole of Greek philosophy endorsing the comparative series: actual, more actual, and most actual. We attempt at least to enter sympathetically into this idea of "enhancement," and we must conclude, without further ado, that the *most actual* must be the *most valuable.* Thus, we view the ultimate determining ground of all gradations of value according to degrees of actuality…But the thought of the enhancement of the actual arises solely from the *images* (allegedly of the so-called external world, although we are in fact referring to images purely and simply, and therefore we include among these images the visions and phantoms of our dreams). Thus, the ultimate ground of all judgments regarding actuality resides in the *images.* (AG p. 151)

TIME AND MEMORY. Through untold millennia stretches the umbilical cord of primal memory; and just as a wine improves with age, so does primal memory send its smoke *higher* the *longer* it has slept in the chthonic urn. (LK GL p. 238)

THE ELEMENTAL VISION. The elemental vision signals rebirth; within us, the element recalls its limitlessness amid the primordial flux, as element and flux devour themselves anew: the winds, the trees, and the stars now speak. Through immeasurably distant ages, death and birth greet the soul of man in the wavering blade of grass, and they hear the dark inner night of the blood of man in the falling rain, as it trickles through the leaves outside. (LK GL p. 239)

THE FIRE OF LIFE. The past is the hearth-fire of life. Every profoundly living being is great only through its origins. (LK GL p. 239)

TIME AND IMAGE. Only that which once occurred can embody itself in the image, and the gaze of the soul is by necessity directed backwards. Out of time's abyss the consciousness of the past breaks into man as the flowering of the elemental powers. (LK GL p. 239)

THE FATE OF THE IMAGES. With every diminution of the elemental past, there is a concomitant decrease in the ability of consciousness to receive the images. Hence, there is a decline in the majesty, depth, and beauty of the images. (LK GL p. 239)

THE ANCIENT SOULS. The present escapes the danger of emptiness only when it is stirred by the primordial images of the past; the moment is only filled to the brim with life when the souls of olden times renew themselves within us. (LK GL p. 239)

THE SOUL AND ITS MOMENTS. Without a connection to the images of times past, the soul's moments would be utterly empty. (LK GL p. 239)

FROM A LETTER WRITTEN DURING THE FIRST WORLD WAR. In millions of hearts those ancient words are shining: *love of the fatherland.* Those words stand for an all-conquering faith, a faith that arouses within us those feelings that are the strongest and deepest ties that bind human society together. Nevertheless, we who — unhappily! — see through words to the facts behind them, know that *the state* has long since usurped the rightful place of the fatherland. We know as well that our victory in this war would only mean the victory of dams, factories, and the Jewish Press. That is the reality of the "German Fatherland!"...And what needs to be said today is this: the blood of our young men is being shed for the spirit of Judaism! (LK GL p. 616)

The Golem as Man of the Future.

The Golem is bound up with the problem of vampirism, for the Golem is but a particular species of vampire...He is, in fact, the "man of the future!" He is that man — or *non-man* — over whom the machine will exercise complete domination. Already, the machine has liberated itself from man's control; it is no longer man's servant: in reality, *man himself is now being enslaved by the machine.* (LK GL p. 678)

Absolute Truth and Relative Truth.

The phenomenon of individual partisanship has nothing whatsoever to do with the question as to the absolute or the relative nature of truth. I consider my fundamental discoveries to be not only absolutely true, but also to be completely demonstrable. I have discussed these matters with the shrewdest thinkers of my time, and yet I have never encountered among them — even among those who were explicitly hostile to my entire philosophical enterprise — anyone who was able to refute even a single judgment of mine. The meaning-content of our judgment is relative, *but only as regards an individual's choice of the party to which he will give his allegiance.* The duality of Spirit and life that I have established is as firmly grounded as any mathematical truth. The only thing that remains in dispute is whether it is more appropriate for an individual to adhere to the party of life or to the party of Spirit. One is free to opt for either party without fear of contradiction. On the other hand, *one can certainly discern the presence of deception as soon as a member of the party of Spirit seeks to deny the existence of the essential disparity between Spirit and life.* (LK GL p. 697)

FROM A LETTER. What you have described as an inner "guide" [*Führer*] recalls to mind the fact that throughout the ancient world we repeatedly encounter the similar phenomenon of the "*Doppelgänger*" — among the Persians it was the "Fravashi;" among the Greeks we find the "eidolon;" and among the Romans we have both the "genius" and the "*numen*." (LK GL p. 698)

"ROMANTIC" AND "CLASSICAL." With regard to the relationship between the "romantic" (or elemental) and the "classical" modes of life-feeling, we admit that the Goethean variety of "self-control" is certainly the most masterful that has been achieved in modern times; but it remains, after all, just that: mere self-control; and we may be sure that this Goethean attitude of *Spirit* will never enable us to reach the elemental reaches of the cosmic horizon of *life*. (LK GL p. 698)

STEWARDS OF THE WORLD. The impulse to guard or protect the world [*Weltgeborgenheit*] is quite similar to our attachment to our family, to our race or nation, to our home-town, to our state, to our species, to our planet, and to our universe, in that the bonds in question constitute real connections and not merely spiritual relationships. Such true connections can only arise between one living being and another, for the connections are themselves are the fundamental forms of all living being. In bygone days we expressed these perceptions through the medium of metaphysics, or, in the vernacular, through religion, so that what we now refer to as world-connection or world-protection binds the individual soul to the world-mystery...Every diminution of this sense of mystery ensures, among other things, that man's activities, his vocation, his pleasures, and in the end his entire life, become devoid of mystery. This accounts for all of the shallowness, the triteness, and the banality of our age; and upon such foundations, the goal-obsessed Mammonism of today has erected its house! (LK GL pp. 1113–4)

HELLENISM. Hellenic measure and Hellenic Eros are one and the same. (RR p. 304)

THE MEANING OF DIALECTIC. Philosophical dialectic thrives on the impulse to transcend conceptual thought. (RR p. 305)

ON REPEATING AN EXPERIENCE. Nothing ever recurs. Each experience is unique and unrepeatable. (RR p. 306)

ORIGIN OF MALICE. Why is this man so quarrelsome and malicious? *He feeds on his envy.* (RR p. 307)

THE POLES OF TIME. The past and the present — and not the past and the future — are the poles of time. (SW 3 p. 434)

ON ETERNITY. Reality exists eternally, and time is the pulse-beat of eternity. (SW 3 p. 435)

POETRY AS LIVING FORM. Poetry is an ecstatic vital force. The life of the poet is an inner poetry. Poetic experience is the magical experience of language. (RR p. 243)

SOUL AND DESTINY. Every soul bears from birth the color of its destiny. It has no need to think clearly about its fate, for it well understands the dream-images of creative ecstasy that shine before it. (RR p. 254)

GROUNDS FOR LOVE. We love only those with whom we share both revelry and grief. (RR p. 256)

FEELING AND LIFE. The most emotional man is not necessarily the most *alive.* (RR p. 256)

THE ELEMENT OF LIFE. Purple and fiery is the living creative element: but it appears as flame in this one, heat in that. (RR p. 256)

THE PHARAOH AND THE "ONE GOD." As an embodiment of the hostility of the allegedly monotheistic, but in actuality *atheistic,* attitude of thought towards the polytheistic vision, the history of religious beliefs provides one instance that, in its immediate, illustrative force, surpasses even the development of Jewish "monotheism." We allude to the attempt of the Egyptian monarch Amenhotep IV, who adopted the name Akhenaton, i.e., "the shining disc of the sun," to overturn the innumerable demonic cults of his people, and to replace them with the worship of the "one true godhead"…

These were the results: on the Pharaoh's side, a bitterly fanatical struggle against all the cultic sites of the polytheists…On the side of the people, whom he had sought to please with his "higher wisdom," a passionate and ever-increasing opposition, which, in just a few years, led to the annihilation of his work, the shattering of his great temples, the consigning of the emperor's teachings to the death of forgotten things, and the reestablishment of an unlimited polytheism, which was to last until the very end of the history of Pharaonic Egypt! (SW 2 p. 1266)

HATE AND THE PROPHETS. The victorious "monotheism" of the prophets of Israel achieved the astonishing trick of raising to the position of personal "lord" of the whole world," purely and simply their own boundless hatred towards the true divinity of this world. (SW 2 p. 1266)

ON THE ENGLISH PHILOSOPHY OF THE "TABULA RASA." If the chick that has only just left the egg immediately pecks at the grain, then without a doubt it has recognized the significance of the grain in serving to satisfy its hunger; similarly the duckling discovers its true element in the water into which — literally without reflection — it dives. The example is often cited of the species of wasp that brings to its larvae certain organisms that it has paralyzed, but not killed, with complicated stings, because they are destined later to serve as living food for its young. Thus the wasp appears to manifest the knowledge of a profoundly schooled anatomist, though, in fact, it cannot possibly have acquired such specialized knowledge. A horse, which has hitherto never encountered a beast of prey, is immediately seized by panic fear when it scents a lion and gallops away in wild flight: thus, the horse recognizes the significance of the scent of the lion, at least with reference to itself. These examples might be multiplied to infinity in order to demonstrate irrefutably the error of the English sensualists when they speak of the soul as of a "blank tablet": for, though the soul bring no impressions with it into the world, it does bring a disposition for the interpretation of the world. These dispositions are commonly referred to as "innate instincts." (SW 4 p. 254)

INNER AND OUTER. Of all of the profound utterances of Novalis, one of the deepest is the following: "The site of the soul is located at the point of connection between the outer world and the inner," and of all the errors that originate in the faith in the actuality of things, one of the most absurd has resulted in the lunatic attempt to locate the "site" of the soul within the anatomy. The contrast of symbolic depth and symbolic surface is justified; but the "road inward" (which is represented in Heraclitus as the "road upward!") is the road leading away from the appearances ("surfaces") and into the depths wherein they appear, and certainly not from the natural exterior of the body to the matter with which it is filled. (SW 2 p. 1141)

ROBBERY AS GOOD BUSINESS. Morality begins with the organizing of theft under the name of trade. Nietzsche may well have been on the right track when he located the source of the idea of justice in the sense of guilt. The recognition that "what is fitting to one is just to another," presupposes an abstraction not only from the inner sentiments, for it also entails an even more fundamental abstraction, the one that establishes the great divide between egoism and racial instinct. It is at this point that man takes the first step beyond racial instinct and into the superstitious belief in "humanity." (RR p. 398)

IMAGES AND SOULS. Every one of my books harbors within it a key thesis; to my sorrow, not one of my readers seems to have been able to discover this secret. The reader may, in fact, be aware of the thesis, but he is somehow blind to the fact that it constitutes the key to the matter in hand!…The key to my book on the "cosmogonic Eros," for instance, is this proposition: *the primordial images are the phenomenal souls of the past.* (LK GL p. 1076)

THE POWER OF THE WORD. One hears a lot of talk about the poverty of language, and it is said that words are inadequate to express our deepest experiences; it is, perhaps, more accurate to speak of a poverty of *experience,* which in countless instances borrows only a semblance of significance from the display of words in which it clothes itself. Life, which has coagulated into speech, in ardor and wildness and in spiritual range leaves far behind the ultimate heights and depths in the life of the individual (apart from the dim feelings of earliest youth); and for this reason alone, it still possesses the power, once it is stirred, to transport the soul even now with an almost supernatural sorcery, carrying it into a whirlpool of more-than-human experience, unattainable otherwise: and a great poet leads us into an unknown magical kingdom, solely because he is blessed with the genius of language. (SW 4 p. 230)

IMAGES ARE NOT IDEAS. Neither the Romantics, with their startling concept of "cosmic consciousness," nor Bachofen, nor Nietzsche, were able to reveal to me that which I would eventually discover for myself: that vision, feeling, and perception, are fundamental functions of the soul, and that these functions, strictly speaking, are analogous to the revelatory activity of the images…But the real danger that must be avoided here is the temptation to confuse these images with the Platonic or neo-Platonic "ideas." (LK GL p. 1073)

ROMANTIC DIALECTICIANS. There is no greater idiocy than the belief that the true mystics and the true Romantics have murky minds.

Precisely the opposite is the case. We find the most rigorous dialecticians, without exception, among the Romantics! (LK GL p. 1078)

LITTLE MAN LUTHER. Had the *petit bourgeois* Luther possessed even a fraction of the radiant understanding of the mystic Meister Eckhart, his "Protestantism" would have been less completely enslaved by the "letter of the law." (LK GL p. 1078)

IMAGINATION AND THE SEXES [FROM A LETTER]. You have said that you are convinced that the soul of woman is dreamier and closer to the images than is the soul of man. In my view, this is completely erroneous. I ask you now to call to mind the truly significant individuals with whom you have come in contact during the course of your life. Ask yourself: all other things being equal, is it man or woman who possesses the larger endowment of imagination? I have been involved for many years with the characterological study of problems relating to the distinctions between the sexes, and I must say: even among the most outstanding women whom I have known, I found none who possesses a consequential power of imagination. Now someone might object that the psychology of women may well have altered since primitive times. I respond: yes, but men have undoubtedly changed to an even greater degree. If you ignore the so-called "emancipated" variety, you will certainly find that, in important matters, contemporary woman more closely resembles her ancestors than contemporary man resembles his forbears. The lack of imagination in women is obvious throughout recorded history, and one must doubt that the situation has changed since prehistoric times. *In the whole of recorded history, there have been only two supremely gifted poetesses: Sappho and Annette von Droste-Hülshoff!* (LK GL pp. 1076–7)

MIND AGAINST LIFE. The awakening of self-consciousness is the declaration of war issued by a hostile god against life. Man is henceforth forever separated from star and storm. (RR p. 423)

"KNOW THYSELF." It is no harmless inscription that looms over the entrance to the shrine at Delphi: this inscription announces the onset of the faith in a transcendent world. Greek life allows itself to be guided by this faith; Pelasgian wisdom perishes at its approach. (RR p. 423)

BACK TO THE ARDOR OF THE PRIMAL SOUL. Burckhardt paved a road back to the immoralism of the Renaissance, where at least part of his nature was content to remain; Bachofen, who belonged to Burckhardt's generation, probed incomparably deeper, and he eventually penetrated all the way back to that chthonic substratum in which the pre-moralistic conception of the world, not merely of the Mediterranean peoples, but the whole of mankind, has its roots. Boecklin captured in the medium of color, and Conrad Ferdinand Meyer fixed in the medium of the word, the spectacle of a primordial world for which, in the end, Nietzsche, who was in large part a successor to these pivotal figures, discovered the symbol that would stand as the emblem of all such visions: he gave it the name of the god of masks, *Dionysus.* (LK GL p. 82)

AUTOBIOGRAPHICAL NOTE. In my youth two essences, the human and the demonic, gathered strength, grew, and matured within me, and they developed without my being able to distinguish one from the other. It was a time of the darkest meditations...of unknowing blessedness, the time of my fullest and deepest experience. It was Peer Gynt before he was torn away from the ardent night of the maternal breast. (LK GL p. 24)

THE POET AND THE GODS. The poet expresses the last tragic flaring up in Western culture of the world of the gods against the "one god" of the Levant. (LK GL p. 51)

MYTH AND SYMBOL. To understand the convictions of a believer one must know the myth out of which they arose; to understand the myth, one must know the symbol that embodies it. To understand the symbol, however, one must know the unique experience that gave birth to it; that type of knowledge can never be mediated by critical judgment. (SW 3 p. 415)

IBSEN AND THE "LIFE-LIE." The young people of today can form no conception of the power of the influence that Ibsen's works had upon the young people of the 1890s. His impact was centered less upon his poetic side, which was only temporarily revealed in his *Peer Gynt*, than it was upon his outspoken battle against those ideological "life-lies," with which the furtive, atomized forces of the latter half of the nineteenth century so colorfully clothed themselves. (LK GL p. 72)

ON GESTURES. The philosophy of antiquity had already divided the expressive phenomena into two significant groups (*significatio* and *gestus scenicus*), and this distinction has recently been revived in our mime and pantomime. The simplest example of pantomime is the gesture of pointing. On the other hand, the majority of expressive movements belong not to the imitative, but to the reflexive or, one might say, *retroactive* processes. (AG p. 114)

A WARNING. I could fill many notebooks with the most precise records of the plundering of my ideas. These acts of theft were certainly not unconscious, but rather blatantly intentional. Now should these burglars continue their activities, the day may come when I will no longer be content to scribble the names of the offenders in private notebooks. At such a time, I will openly publish these records, naming names and unmasking the vileness of the thieves' methods. Then everyone will be able to see with crystal clarity that this sort of robbery is not merely systematic, but it is also characteristic of the misdeeds of a certain racial element. What we're dealing with here is something far greater than the robbing of one individual. In fact what I have discovered might even be said to constitute a significant contribution to the history of the "culture of the modern age"; this tale might also serve as a revelation of the furtive procedures adopted by envious souls. Publication will certainly startle more than one or two of these clever connoisseurs! (SW 2 pp. 1535–6)

BENJAMIN FRANKLIN. From Franklin's autobiography we learn that this man, who discovered and popularized the slogan "Time is money," in the course of his life established thirteen "virtues," the last of which, "humility," is relevant to his aforementioned proposition regarding time and money. All of his so-called virtues orbit around one particular virtue: *thrift*. One has to exercise thrift in one's eating, drinking, sexual intercourse, movements, words, tasks, feelings, time, etc. For Franklin, "virtue" means every quality and form of personal conduct that can serve to promote the Spirit of thrift and keep that Spirit before the eyes of one's fellow earthlings. Franklin represents the achievement of a type, viz., that of the *homme clos,* of the man whose personal character is covered over, in approximate accord with the following scheme: purpose = the accumulation of cash ("Mammon"); the mediator of that purpose: thrift, systematized upon a daily and even hourly basis = the methodical adjustment of all impulses, inclinations, and wishes towards the sacred goal of profit. In other words: the first, second, and third precept is *taking,* whilst *giving* might be indulged in only to the extent that it will result in greater profits in the long run!

By the middle of the eighteenth century, Franklin's *The Road to Riches* had been translated into sixteen languages, including Chinese. For all of these reasons, we place Franklin at the head of the pack of early capitalists. As we can see from his notebooks, with their embarrassingly exact division of the working day (comprising both spoken and written efforts), he lays claim to just six hours for his own uses. That would be a scandalous waste of time from the standpoint of a representative of the later phase of "high" capitalism…And certainly Franklin's attitude towards Mammon shows us that he is merely a pathfinder for those who would one day reduce life to the level of a "prosperous" and "care-free" existence…

During the phase of high capitalism, man is finally to be converted into a mere economic function. (SW 5 p. 485)

ANCIENT RECORDS. Among the remains of ancient peoples there are no documentary records of the inner life that can match speech for sheer strength and directness; but this document cannot evade the necessity for psychological interpretation. Consciousness has crystallized in innumerable shapes, and all that is required of the student is a clear eye in order for him to be able to "read" in buildings, ornaments, and images, the confirmation and the complement of the evidence that actions historically vouched-for can furnish regarding the characterology of their authors. There is available here such a mass of material as never yet was the property of any science, and we would already be in the certain possession of the vastest knowledge, if only our historians possessed that psychological amazement that raises, whenever we are faced with any kind of form, work, or type of activity, the right questions as to what might be the forces that have produced these things. For the first time, customs, sagas, and conceptions of gods, costumes, and household articles, languages and systems of writing, can, and must, be interrogated deliberately, without any preconceived notions as to their origins. These data are to be understood; and, being understood, they will aid us in the completion of our picture of man. (SW 4 236)

THE GATES OF DEATH. To my mind death is the ultimate fulfillment of life, and whether it is the song of a human voice or the stormwind as it uproots the forest that opens the gates of death, it is all one to me. (RR p. 522)

EROS COSMOGONOS. Eros is not just a fine, blind, animalistic sensuality; we must be more precise: Eros is sensuality at the very moment of its realization. He who is inhabited by Eros-Dionysus becomes a demon whilst he yet remains a man. Such a man sees through the shadow-body of things into the flaming night of the images. He himself is destiny; he himself incarnates a Medusean dread. The streams of earth, the storms of heaven, and the starry vault above are all within him, and his power reaches beyond the orbit of Saturn. (RR p. 523)

Towards a Pagan Metaphysics. A pagan metaphysical system would not be philosophy as one understands that word today, i.e., the hair-splitting rehashing of such life-alien concepts as would be appropriate to the lecture hall; nor would it be characterized by that sort of factitious profundity that seeks to conceal its utter inability to solve the riddles of thought behind a veil of second-rate poetic fables. Neither should a genuine pagan metaphysics resemble that which passes for science in the modern world, for science, in spite of its outstanding achievements, is in danger of becoming the mere discovery in cognition of truths which may be necessary, but which are also, considered from the standpoint life, utterly unimportant. Before we can discover truths that go to the very roots, we must possess a greater fund of inwardness than can be discerned in those thinkers who, for at least the last five hundred years, have expended their energies exclusively within the realm of *reason*. (RR p. 373)

On the Will and its Suppression of the Emotions. The so-called capacity of the will constitutes a capacity for suppressing the emotions, or more briefly, a capacity for self-control; but we must also bear in mind that self-control at certain times serves to realize external events of volition, and at other times it operates for its own sake. The self-mastery that a "saint," a "Yogi," or any other ascetic requires, great as it undoubtedly is, nevertheless is still a very different matter from the self-control that a Napoleon needs on a thousand occasions in order to realize his plans for conquest. (SW 4 p. 228)

On the Panoramic Enormity of the Mountain Range. These rigid peaks of ice invite comparison with the deeds of a world-conqueror: harsh and inexorable, dreadful, radiating an iron, unfeeling lack of soul. The mountain range, from its bottommost stratum to its loftiest heights, has no soul.

How different is the sea: where the elemental soul *lives*. (LK GL p. 131)

A PHILOSOPHER (WITH A DOCTORATE IN CHEMISTRY) REFLECTS ON SCIENCE. Every science has to achieve clarity regarding that which it must do, by pondering from the loftiest perspective that which it *can* do. That even now we cannot express chemical processes in terms of physical equations is transparently clear. But it is equally certain that at least 75% of all the discoveries of modern science are completely without significance. The annual publication of new compounds shows that in most cases the results of our research have not the slightest importance. It is merely mendacious to claim that these trivial discoveries constitute interim stages on the high road to truly significant syntheses. No one has even come close to convincing us of the truth of that point of view! We produce according to the yardstick of traditional and readily accessible methods a superabundance of material whose existence (or non-existence) has no scientific value whatsoever. (The results that have been exploited by technological concerns, of course, are divorced from the realm of true science.) Thus, we are led to the conclusion that for all of our active scientists (especially our "great" organic chemists of today) the authentic goals of true science have been utterly lost. (LK GL p. 147)

A PROPHECY (FROM 1897). The culture of Europe is about to be devoured by Pan-Slavic barbarism; thereupon will follow a fight to the death between Slavic and Mongol hordes; ultimately, the crucial battle will be fought between the European continent and an ascendant America.

Fragments of our intuitive culture may be rescued, but in all likelihood such remnants will be scarcely more comprehensible to posterity than ancient Egypt is to us today. (LK GL p. 161)

HONORING THE DEAD. Nothing seems to have been regarded as of greater importance to the ancient Pelasgians, than the solemnity with which they conducted their funerary rites and the great care which they bestowed upon the mortal remains. The most overwhelming dramatic creation of the entire ancient world celebrates the heroic self-sacrifice of Antigone, who so tenderly obeyed her sacred duty when she buried her fallen brothers. This theme is certainly without peer, especially if we measure it against the "poetry" of our own days!

Originally, those ancient interments were probably within the house, perhaps beneath the hearth-fire. In later days, the remains were laid to rest in the very center of the village. Then, they were placed before the city walls or city gates; eventually the dead were buried somewhere in the marketplace, or in the Prytaneum, or in the plaza of the polis. Thus, at Olympia we find the grave of Pelops alongside the great altar that was dedicated to Zeus; and these burial-sites were always venerated as being the burial chambers of demons. (One example must suffice: the temple of Apollo at Delphi was constructed atop the crypt of the mother-goddess Python.)...

Tombs were always regarded as holy, for they were often no less than the "sacred grove" or the "blessed mountain" of so many peoples: the Manitou-stone of the Amerindians, the pagodas of the Chinese, and the stupas of the culture of the Indian sub-continent, are just a few examples of this phenomenon. The souls of the dead floated and soared above and around the gravestones, which were oftentimes carved in the likeness of a great serpent, who dwelt therein as the *genius loci*, the Agatho-demon, who endlessly dispenses blessings upon *the house of the living.*

The entire culture of the ancient Romans recalled their primordial roots when they honored their domestic ancestral spirits, the "Lares," just as the Shintoists in Japan honor their own ancestors even now. The nations of antiquity, along with the so-called "primitive" cultures that have survived into our own times, all bestow homage upon the noble dead.

From this honoring of the dead there arose the Hellenic *Agon,* which is a sensual and visible commemoration of the endless cycle of coming to be and passing away. We must understand that these peoples were not filled with dread of ghosts from whom they assiduously sought to protect themselves; instead, we perceive the loving respect tendered by all of those now living as they, expressing a different form of love, enroll the newly deceased on the honor-roll that bears the names of the noble figures of the

past. These customs are enshrined in cultic rites, some of which are immediately comprehensible, while others seems to signify certain profoundly
significant mysteries: but all such rituals reveal that the celebrants regard
the deceased as forever standing "within life!" (SW III pp. 443–4)

MATTER AND IMAGE. The school of thought that portrays matter
as the substratum that supports the world of perception is merely con-
cocting a "thought-thing" [*Gedankending*], and this false teaching was
devised, of course, to advance Spirit's all-conquering impulse to subject
physical movements to the rule of a quantifying formalism. Matter, considered as the habitation of the images (the very word "matter" betrays
the fact), attempts to inhabit a dark hemisphere of actuality, a realm that,
without the living light of phenomenal appearances, would be utterly un-
thinkable. (SW III p. 459)

THE PERFECTED ECSTASY. In the rush of ecstasy, life seeks to lib-
erate itself from the chains of Spirit. Perfection is achieved when the soul
awakens, and the awakened soul is *vision*. What is revealed is the actuality
of the primordial images. *The primordial images are the phenomenally appearing souls of the past.* (SW III p. 470)

IMAGE AND THING. We formulate the following dualities: The image has presence only in the instant during which it is experienced. The
thing is "established" once and for all.

The image passes away, just as experience passes away. The thing is
rigidly fixed, enduring, standing always in life-alien enmity.

The image is only there in the experience as it is lived. The thing is an
arbitrary percept available to anyone.

In the image I can summon to my recollection something from the
vanished immemorial past; however, I cannot incorporate that memory
in a spontaneous judgment. With regard to the thing, since it is now ex-
actly what it is at any time, and in any space, I can always comprehend

a thing, and by means of my critical judgment, I can arrive at identical reference points that are quite sufficient for general purposes.

The image, deeply connected to the stream of time, transforms itself, as it transforms everything that is esteemed by the living soul. The thing, since it is outside the realm of time, collapses, fittingly, into utter destruction.

The image is received by the soul. The thing runs aground through the critical activity of Spirit.

The image is independent of conscious reality. The thing is a concept in the world of consciousness, and exists solely for the inner life of a discrete person.

So: Whoever shatters his personal existence in order to embark on an attempt to experience true ecstasy will discover, in that very moment, that the world of facts has perished, and that there has arisen within him all the overwhelming force of a now-vibrant actuality. This actuality is the world of the images. The visionary soul is its inner pole, whilst the appearing actuality is its outer pole…

Recall the words of Novalis: "The outer world is only an inner one that has been raised to the condition of secrecy." (SW III pp. 416–7)

ON TRUTH AND ACTUALITY. From time immemorial, the vexed question regarding a general criterion of truth has remained unanswerable, as any proposed solution would presuppose the validity of that which is in question. It is also unnecessary that we establish such a criterion, since there are numerous propositions, both factual and philosophical, that possess such inherently compelling force that we habitually refer to them as "immediately self-evident." Still, it is crucial that we understand that the expressions "true" and "false" pertain only to our judgments. In a world wherein there existed no thinking consciousness, such predicates would be utterly devoid of meaning.

Even if all of the discrete sciences should decide to co-ordinate their efforts so as to achieve one universal science that would be based upon correct and incontrovertible judgments, there would still be two opposed camps within that one scientific discipline when it came to the question regarding the actuality-content of scientific judgments. The first group would explain as mere objects of thought that which the other camp would hold to be actuality itself; one group would see mere appearance in that which the other considered to be genuine substance. The one camp (which today constitutes the majority party) again falls into two sub-divisions, known as "idealists" and "materialists." The school of idealists, whose founding father is Plato, insists that the ultimate realities are concepts ("ideas," "representations"). The school of materialists, whose founding father is Democritus, hold that concepts are merely propositions that have been designed so as to correspond with objects. Above all, however, objects are objects of thought, which we comprehend with the aid of concepts: thus, both parties endorse the faith in the creative, or the formative, power of the (human) spirit, the idealist consciously, the materialist (for the most part) unconsciously. Therefore, we call the camp of the majority, comprising both the "idealist" and the "realist," the logocentric school.

The minority party, the party of opposition, we call the biocentric school. Its representatives look upon the matters in question as follows: all the proper objects of thought, both those mediated by thought and those immediately given, arise out of the sphere of actuality, but they do not contain actuality; for actuality can only be experienced, never conceived. Likewise, an understanding of the actual is certainly possible, but this understanding can never be exhaustively explained or conceptualized. The science of actuality is the science of appearances; the science of appearances strives to achieve a profound comprehension of the content of experience. Its aim is the discovery of that which Goethe referred to as "primal phenomena," in which the meaning of the world reveals itself...

Suppose that two individuals were successively to count the same one hundred dollars, and suppose also that one of the two had been born blind. Now these individuals' perceived images of the marks would easily be distinguished from each other. However, that also holds true, if to a lesser degree, of the perceived images experienced by every living being; indeed, this also holds true of the perceived images in one and the same bearer of perception in different moments of his life. It follows that experiences can never be identically repeated.

In our judgments, we do not perceive reds or blues or colors as generalities; nor do we perceive sounds, tastes, and tactile sensations as generalities; nor do we perceive feelings of thirst or hunger, feelings of hope, yearning and expectation as generalities. What our judgments of the world do achieve in fact is this and this alone: we distinguish the multiform qualities, outer as well as inner, from each other. The qualities are thereby presupposed in the experiences. Our conceptions are derived from the qualities, since the conceptions are abstracted from the vital experience that is received. Whoever regards the objects of thought as actuality, confuses the boundaries that divide the objects with that which has established those boundaries. Conceptual thought must yield place to referential thought. The science of appearances, or the science of actuality, is the science not of conscious thought, but of referential thought.

In the major work of the author of these lines, *Spirit as Adversary of the Soul,* we present the proof of our contention that the objects of thought, both in the "idealist" and the "materialist" incarnations, cannot render the appearances according to their true nature. In every idealist philosopher we have a demonstration that the idealist's own principles render him incapable of distinguishing the world of perceptions from the world of representations. As a result, the idealist must perforce disavow the world of actuality; as a result, that world will always be found to play a miniscule role in the idealist's system. In fact, the idealist treats the world of perception as if it were a product of spiritual activity, whereas this activity could not raise itself up as the antithetical counterpart to the world of perception unless it had based itself upon a previously-existent substratum of vital events.

However, our experiences have no connection with the being-concept, nor have they any true relationship to the kindred existence-concept. For our experiences transform themselves without interruption; to employ the phrase of Heraclitus, they transpire in an "eternal flux." Actuality can neither be conceptualized nor quantified; only that being in which Spirit subdues actuality can be thus rigidly fixed in concept and quantity.

As soon as one is convinced that the substance of experienced life is outside the reach of Spirit, one is compelled to endorse the conviction that conceptualizing Spirit, which is only found in man, is a force that, in-itself and for-itself, does not belong to the cosmos. One can indeed marvel at the deeds that Spirit, employing our activity, has consummated in this world; but one can nevermore fall into the error of attributing creativity to Spirit. Spirit broadens the scope of man's will to power until we come to realize that Spirit unmasks itself as the will to annihilate nature. It is, thus, "utilitarian," and this is the reason why the "truths" of the party of Spirit have seduced a greater number of disciples than can ever be found in the party of life. "Knowledge," in the biocentric sense, is seen as an end in itself. Such knowledge is only sought by the chosen few, who regard every glimpse into the nature of actuality as more rewarding than the fruits of utilitarianism and the will to power. (SW III pp. 720–22)

OTHER BOOKS PUBLISHED BY ARKTOS

OTHER BOOKS PUBLISHED BY ARKTOS

PORUS HOMI HAVEWALA — *The Saga of the Aryan Race*

RACHEL HAYWIRE — *The New Reaction*

LARS HOLGER HOLM — *Hiding in Broad Daylight*
Homo Maximus
The Owls of Afrasiab

ALEXANDER JACOB — *De Naturae Natura*

PETER KING — *Keeping Things Close: Essays on the Conservative Disposition*

LUDWIG KLAGES — *The Biocentric Worldview*

PIERRE KREBS — *Fighting for the Essence*

PENTTI LINKOLA — *Can Life Prevail?*

H. P. LOVECRAFT — *The Conservative*

BRIAN ANSE PATRICK — *The NRA and the Media*
Rise of the Anti-Media
The Ten Commandments of Propaganda
Zombology

TITO PERDUE — *Morning Crafts*

RAIDO — *A Handbook of Traditional Living*

STEVEN J. ROSEN — *The Agni and the Ecstasy*
The Jedi in the Lotus

RICHARD RUDGLEY — *Barbarians*
Essential Substances
Wildest Dreams

OTHER BOOKS PUBLISHED BY ARKTOS

Made in the USA
Las Vegas, NV
09 January 2025

16163628R00114